"I love wh
especially   ; in
his own life and ministry. . . . .   like
this to encourage me toward this type of ministry years
ago, but I'm deeply thankful that it's now out there to
encourage future missionaries to the 'uncool' places to
do ministry that doesn't look like church work alone.
The truth is that this type of ministry thinking will soon
be necessary if we're to continue to engage deeply as
Christians in the United States."

Andy Littleton

Pastor of Mission Church and Owner of
Midtown Artisans in Tucson, AZ

"I've long been a fan of anything and everything Benesh
writes. He's a voice in the desert, a clarion call to what's
coming. It's time to make way for how God wants to
come into our communities, and *Intrepid* is like a
highway. The fact that Benesh is a thinking practitioner
gives him an edge in the conversation and makes this
book worth paying attention to."

Peyton Jones

Author of Reaching The
Unreached and Church Zero

"I believe Sean has truly tapped into a kingdom-focused
view of missional church planting. This is not just
another book about the trends of 'business as mission'
or 'church planting as tent making.' It goes deeper,
farther, bigger, and requires so much more. This book
goes to the heart of what it means to be a sent one of
God. Sean makes the appropriate distinction between

'missions' (over there) and 'ministry' (here). He dispels common myths about America as a mission field, and makes a clear and compelling case for how church planters can provide for their families, create an engaged community and bless their cities through social entrepreneurship. If you read one book on church planting, read this one."

Jonathan Chambers

Community Manager of Entrepreneurship,
Cherokee Office of Economic Development,
Woodstock, GA

In *Intrepid*, Sean Benesh takes a fresh look at the age-old struggle of how those in ministry can support themselves while building the kingdom. Sean's innovative approach goes a step further than 'tent-making,' demonstrating how church planters can be catalysts for holistic transformation in fragile communities. Sean will expand your thinking on the purpose and methods of church planting, demonstrating practical ways church planters can creatively bring the whole gospel to communities. Those who plant churches are entrepreneurs at heart. Sean's approach provides an inspiring blueprint to channel that entrepreneurship into sharing the gospel in word, in deed, and to empower human flourishing.

Beth Sethi

MBA, Nonprofit Capacity Builder
and Adjunct Professor of Global
Development, Multnomah University

INTREPID

SEAN BENESH

Intrepid
Navigating the Intersection of Church Planting + Social Entrepreneurship

Published by Missional Challenge Publishing
www.missionalchallenge.com

Missional Challenge
PUBLISHING

ISBN 13: 978-1-939921-86-4

Manufactured in the U.S.A

CONTENT

Foreword

Interest in church planting has skyrocketed over the past decade. As a result of declining attendance and the closing of many existing churches, every major denomination is focusing more resources toward starting new congregations. We have also seen the creation of multiple church planting networks that emphasize church planting across denominational lines.

In the midst of this proliferation of new church startups, a significant trend is the starting of new churches by bi-vocational leaders. Historically the phrase "bi-vocational pastor" referred to a leader who served a church that was unable to compensate a pastor with a full-time salary. Therefore, the pastor would work a second or third job to supplement the salary the church could provide. This was mostly out of necessity rather than preference. Often the term "tentmaker" (the Apostle Paul's trade described in Acts 18) has been used to define this type of church planter.

Today, there is a new movement of bi-vocational leaders. These church planters are *choosing* to plant bi-vocationally with the conviction that bi-vocational church planting actually provides a more desirable way to plant a new church (it's no longer embraced simply as a

i

solution to limited funds). In other words, bi-vocational church planting is becoming a first option, not a last resort.

However, what excites me most about this fresh interest in bi-vocational church planting is that it gives planters the imagination to rethink what it means to plant a church. Planters are recognizing that as we do ministry in an increasingly missionary context, we must move beyond traditional church planting approaches. Historically, church planting methodology has been primarily about "launching" a Sunday morning worship service. While there may still be a place for this approach in some pockets of North America, those contexts are decreasing rapidly. We desperately need a fresh vision for church planting in a post-Christendom context.

That brings me to this latest book by Sean Benesh. Not only does Sean provide this new imagination needed for church planting—that focuses on Kingdom ventures that partner with what God is already doing in a city—but he challenges planters to see themselves as church planting missionaries rather than pastors starting worship services. He paints a beautiful picture of the interplay between mission, social entrepreneurship, community restoration and church planting.

What Sean is proposing will help to mobilize the planting of new churches across North America in under-reached and off-the-beaten-path communities, particularly communities that have been in economic decline and are transitioning to revitalize their local economy. Consider the impact of churches planted where people come to Christ and the community is lifted up through new businesses, non-profits, job creation, and more. If you desire to see genuine and long-lasting community impact, then you must read what Sean is suggesting, and step into the adventure with both feet.

Brad Brisco

Director of Bi-vocational Church Planting for the North American Mission Board and author of *The Missional Quest* and *Next Door as It Is in Heaven*

Preface

Why, you may ask, do we need another book about church planting, bi-vocationalism, start-ups, and social entrepreneurship? Or maybe you're thinking to yourself, "What does this guy even know about these topics? What qualifies him to write on this?" Excellent and valid questions.

Maybe since I'm combining church planting with social entrepreneurship, then the line of questions that follows is: Am I or have I ever been a church planter? Am I an entrepreneur? My answers ought to get to the heart of whether I'm competent in those arenas or not.

My journey into both areas happened more by simply operating out of my default mode than anything else, interwoven with a sense of calling and knowing how God has wired me. I know I'm wired to create things from scratch. That doesn't mean I'm the best at it, nor will I ever claim to be. I create because it's who I am. Church planting, business start-ups, writing books, and the like flow out of this.

My life has revolved around church planting for the last fifteen years. I love church planters. They are my biggest heroes. More than simply pastors starting new congregations from scratch, they are ultimately missionaries. Church planters do what they do because they are compelled by the *missio Dei*. Many lay it literally all on the line to engage in this start-up work. They leave hometowns, sell homes, move across the city, county, or globe to do this. In the truest sense, they pick up their crosses, die to self, and follow Christ.

Within any industry, occupation, or discipline there are outliers or disruptors who break from the norm to do something fresh and new. There is a disruption currently taking place within church planting. Part of it is centered on this notion of bi-vocationalism. This goes beyond the need for church planters to work at jobs they hate to pay the bills while they're planting. It's also more than simply making money. More and more church planters, who are by nature entrepreneurial, are thinking about and asking how to work in industries or start something that not only carries them financially, but is actually part of the church-planting process.

This is why I'm writing *Intrepid*. Admittedly I was a subpar church planter and while I've now started two businesses, they're not providing me with an early retirement plan or a third home in southern France. I created both of those start-ups because I was curious and needed a creative outlet. Having gone through the process I've learned much about myself, branding, and connecting with more people.

My hope is that this book will stimulate your thinking about how creative start-ups have a place alongside church planting, and how the two are actually complimentary in many ways.

Where does the name *Intrepid* come from? A quick online search reveals that "intrepid" means something along the lines of "fearless, bold, adventurous, undaunted, indomitable" and the like. That resonates. Intrepid is the perfect descriptor of this new-but-old breed of entrepreneurial church planters who are boldly carving a niche in the church planting world.

Introduction

Whenever I'm getting ready to travel to another city, I'll often spend the night before I leave scouring the internet for good local coffee shops. My options are either to choke down bad coffee somewhere, pack my travel coffee kit (portable travel kettle, grinder, Aeropress, etc.), or actually find a solid cup of coffee at a local roaster. Living in Portland, Oregon, can sometimes spoil me since good coffee cannot be found everywhere. However, as more and more Third Wave coffee roasters start up all across the country, finding good coffee, even in smaller towns, is getting easier.

Last month before I jumped on a plane for Colorado Springs, I looked over a few coffee shop websites, read the pertinent info, and determined much of what to expect based upon the quality of each website, its imagery, and so on. When I arrived, since I had half a day before the conference started, I headed straight to one coffee shop. I showed up at Switchback Roasters.

On one wall was a roastery full of burlap bags of green beans, a Probat coffee roaster, five-gallon buckets, and an assortment of other tools and items needed for a small commercial roaster. On the other side was the coffee shop which was full of patrons, mostly younger adults, but with a few young families sprinkled in. It was a cool spot and a great hub for the neighborhood. I observed lots of conversations and connections taking place.

I walked up to the counter and ordered an El Salvador coffee for a pour-over. After a couple of minutes, with cup in hand, I sat down at the bar next to the espresso machine. It was a good perch from which to get the lay of the land as I checked emails and looked over my notes for the conference. With big windows at my back, a spacious interior that was spot-on in terms of decor, and an amazing cup of coffee, I couldn't but help feel a little smug that my online research for a good coffee shop and roaster had paid off. After an hour or so I packed up, checked into my hotel room, and then went to the conference that night.

With thoughts of the coffee shop fresh in my mind, I made my way to the Ivywild School. A former elementary school turned restaurant, brewery, gathering space, and more, this was a great venue for the pre-conference kick-off. As the event began, many of us were seated around large round tables where discussions were taking place related to different topics on church planting. It was there that I ran into Brandon. We connected immediately because he had moved to Portland for seminary only to return to Colorado Springs after graduation. We had a couple of mutual friends and acquaintances.

But as the conversation progressed, what I learned about Brandon was shockingly awesome... he was the owner of Switchback Roasters. My jaw hit the floor. And to top it off, he was a church planter through the Christian and Missionary Alliance.

Two days later I met Brandon for coffee at Switchback and got to hear the story of coffee roasting and church planting and how they tie together. I also learned what is paramount to the trajectory and scope of this book: 1) His business is able to supplement his income as a church planter, and 2) Because of his business, he is able to consider planting in a part of the city and in a demographic that is lower income.

Meaning that because of his passion and expertise as a roaster, he has not only created a missionary platform from which to launch a church, but he has created a natural gathering place and relational hub for the community. And because of the income it generates, he is "free" to attempt to plant a church among lower-income residents, a group often overlooked in church planting.

There are several reasons why I was drawn to Brandon's story. First of all, I've been gathering research, data, and content for this book for a couple of years now. I have received church-planting training materials from denominations and organizations across the US and Canada. I am interested to see *how* church planters are being trained and, more importantly, *what* they're being trained to do. Is it simply "soft skills" like preaching, discipleship, leading, etc., or is there more? Are planters being trained to think and act like the Brandons out there?

Second, whenever I'm working on a book, it becomes like a filter which life, ministry, and information pass through. In other words, I am keenly aware whenever I see, hear, or learn something that relates to this book. My antennae are always up. Therefore, when I first connected with Brandon, I knew I had to learn more. Why did he choose to go this route? What are the advantages? The disadvantages?

The last reason why Brandon's story caught my attention, apart from the fact that I love coffee, is that I'm wired to be creative and to start stuff. I do not self-identify as an "entrepreneur" nor will I ever, but I know I'm hard-wired to start things, to create. Before I came to Christ, I was an art major in college. Since then I've started a church-planting training center, a publishing company, a coffee-roasting company, and in the same vein have been involved in church planting. Church planting to me is a very creative endeavor where you're starting something from scratch.

All of these interests and experiences coalesced to motivate me to write this book. How are we training our church planters? Are we stuck in old paradigms where we simply look at church planting as an occupation? Or is it a calling? The answer to that question reveals *a lot.* It also informs *how* one goes about church planting.

My goal throughout this book is to present information, challenge assumptions, and poke and prod. But not out of angst or frustration. Rather, my ultimate goal is to elevate church planting as a truly missionary endeavor, more than a career change. You see, when we combine church planting with a missionary mindset here on our "home turf," it begins changing the rules of church planting as well as other related topics such as planting sustainable churches, planting in undesirable places and among marginalized populations, and living out the implications of the gospel.

Let's begin unpacking all of this …

1

THE GOSPEL
IN THE DESERT

+ + + + + + + + + + + + +

The older I get the more I learn about myself. You'd think that because I live inside my own head I'd have a good idea by now of who I am and what I'm like. The irony is that I continue to discover new things about how God has wired me.

This has come to light in the past couple of years. Whenever I become overwhelmed and the stress seems unbearable, I slowly disengage. I usually attempt to distance myself from the source of the tension. At times that means relationally disengaging as well. The problem of late, though, was that this was tied to some of the ideas, topics, and activities that I have loved deeply. Not only that, but when your inner angst and need to disengage pertains to your ministry or livelihood it becomes troublesome. But I had this strong urge to pull away.

This is all part of Burnout 101. What my revulsion turned towards was the city. Living in it became a source of frustration. My love for it waned; nor did I find joy in reading, writing, researching, or reflecting on the city. It used to be that all-things urban were intoxicating. I couldn't get enough. But I became mentally and emotionally fried from teaching, writing, and doing so much training about the city that I needed a reprieve. A mental vacation.

In the midst of this season, I recalled a five-year stretch when I worked as a hiking and mountain-biking guide in southern Arizona. I relived memories of exploring the desert backcountry on foot, in the car, and by mountain bike alone and with my family. During that time, I had devoured a large amount of reading material seeking to understand the desert more deeply, from the local flora and fauna to the storyline of human history in the region. I was a dry sponge absorbing massive amounts of information that I would later recall while hiking and biking on the trail with out-of-state guests.

Dry River

I needed to stop reading about urban planning, economics, creative-class theory, gentrification, and all other related topics. I needed to stop thinking about the rent hikes happening all around the city center that were displacing families. We lived (and still do) in the path of this real estate storm. So instead, I ordered a couple of books that dealt with the history of southern Arizona. This was when I came across the book *Dry River: Stories of Life, Death, and Redemption on the Santa Cruz* by Ken Lamberton.

Its premise is pretty straightforward. Lamberton walks most of the length of the Santa Cruz River and not only documents his journey, but masterfully pulls in figures that once walked and lived along the same stretches. In each chapter, Lamberton introduces the reader to a portion of this small river that has played a significant role in the human history of the area.

The river starts south of Tucson on the southern flank of the Santa Rita mountains where it begins a tenuous journey southward into Mexico. Only a short distance across the border, the river bends sharply north and reenters the United States. It continues north, coming alongside the western edge of the city of Tucson. Further up toward Phoenix, it joins the Gila River only to intermittently flow westward to merge with the Colorado River at the California border. From there it heads south, spilling into the Sea of Cortez. That's the plan at least, since most of the time, except for a brief period after the monsoon rains, it truly is a dry river.

Father Kino

It is along a stretch of the river in northern Mexico, in the small village of Santa Cruz, where we're first introduced to Father Eusebio Francisco Kino. Kino established the original Jesuit mission in that village in 1693. For those who live in or have visited Tucson and southern Arizona, you more than likely have come across the name Kino. Today there are numerous places named after Kino—a sports complex, a parkway, schools, and more. It is a familiar name to residents. But who was he and why does his story matter in a book about church planting?

History is an interesting subject. Quite often key figures, events, and whole tribes or races have been completely forgotten. Or if they are not completely forgotten, they have at least left us without much in the way of documentation that would clue us into what transpired. But then a discovery is made, and suddenly we're reintroduced to these people and events which have long since faded from memory. That's what happened with Kino. Historian Herbert Eugene Bolton penned these words in the 1930s:

> Notable among historical revivals in North America is the new interest in Father Kino, the incomparable pioneer of the Southwest and the Pacific Coast. Famed among his contemporaries and eulogized by his successors, he gradually dropped from view. Then one day his autobiography was discovered in a dusty archive. The precious manuscript, lost for a century and a half, revealed an astounding personage. Slowly, as the account was read, Kino's recreated figure rose above the historical horizon; then suddenly, and as if by a common burst of insight, his significance was grasped.[1]

The story of Father Kino was and is intriguing on many fronts. From his impact in what was then

---

[1] Bolton, *The Padre on Horseback*, 1.

known as Pimería Alta (northern Mexico and southern Arizona) among the Pimas to his introduction of different farming techniques, his presence has cast a long shadow. But what struck me was his missionary training and how he was equipped to be a pioneer church planter. After reading scant accounts in books and online, I picked up Bolton's short work on Kino, *The Padre on Horseback.*

Dangerous Calling

Born in 1645 in Segno, a tiny village in northern Italy, Eusebio Kino (his original surname was Chini) grew up working on his parents' farm. He left for college in Innsbruck, Austria, where he studied rhetoric and logic. Early on, "he showed a propensity for mathematics, but it would be his skills with language and even farming that would be most helpful to him, for it seemed that God had placed a calling upon his life––Kino only needed to realize it."[2] From these accounts it appears that God was preparing him for something that would not only define his life, but also impact generations across the ocean in North America.

A life-altering event took place during college that changed the trajectory of Kino's life.

While in college in Innsbruck, he fell ill and came close to death. He prayed to Saint Francis Xavier for his recovery,

---

[2] Lamberton, *Dry River*, 52-54.

vowing that he would dedicate himself to God and become a Jesuit if he lived. He kept the promise. In 1667 at the age of twenty-two, Kino pronounced his first vows. For another decade he studied mathematics, philosophy, geography, cartography, and astronomy at the Jesuit college in Ingolstadt, Bavaria.[3]

So far Kino's storyline sounds very similar to many of us in full-time ministry. Usually there was a moment, whether a sense that God was speaking to us or a near-tragic event, that God used to move us in the direction that we're on right now. Many of us can relate to Kino. I know I can.

I think it is safe to say that my life was headed nowhere fast as I was graduating from high school. Like many of my peers, I was asking the questions: Where will I to go to college? (Something I should have figured out by then.) What am I going to study? More importantly, what am I going to do for the rest of my life?

Up until that point my life had been significantly impacted by the arts, and in particular by my high school art teacher, Mr. Masters. He was the most influential person in my life and took me under his wing in many ways. Alcoholism had ravaged my relationship with my father, so Mr. Masters was almost my surrogate

---

[3] Ibid., 54.

dad. And not just for me, but for many others as well.

Mr. Masters had a wonderful way of believing in people. I'm not even sure I was that great of an artist, but I was slowly moving in the direction of studying art in college and making art my life's trajectory. I had looked at all kinds of art schools from the Minneapolis College of Art to the Art Institute of Chicago. However, paralyzed with indecision (and a girlfriend) I opted to enroll at a local community college as an art major.

But that summer, in between graduating from high school and going to college, the miraculous happened. In the midst of my deep longing and anguish, I met the person of Jesus.

After my transforming encounter with God, my whole life changed. Not only was I a new creation in Christ, but something, or Someone, beckoned me to dedicate my life to God. I had no idea what that meant, nor did I have any categories or labels for it. I didn't know about "callings" or anything like that. All I knew was that before God had redeemed me, my life was a wreck. But once God intervened, all I could do was think of how grateful I was and how I wanted nothing else than to give my life back in service to God. But I didn't know what that looked like.

During my first year at the local community college, someone suggested I look at a Christian college to pursue this calling. That was a whole category of schooling that I knew nothing about, so I began picking up magazines and catalogs (this was pre-internet, mind you). Over time I narrowed my options to schools in the Midwest.

Within a year I was enrolled at a Christian college studying the Bible, learning theology, and preparing for a life of ministry. I recall arriving on campus with a remedial understanding of Scripture at best. I can relate to Kino because God changed both of our life directions during university, although my experience was not of the near-death variety.

Looking Back to Look Forward

Like Kino, I too can relate to how God has used my past for his service. As we will get into soon, God used Kino's earlier education and experiences (farming) mightily on the mission field. As I mentioned earlier, before I transferred to a Christian college to study for a life of ministry, I started off my collegiate career as an art major. And since I'm wired to create and start things from scratch, I can look back over my life and see how God was preparing me to be involved in church planting and missionary endeavors. It is art for me to help launch new churches from scratch.

Fourteen years after his calling, Kino arrived in New Spain, in Vera Cruz, Mexico. He arrived with the same mindset as many other Jesuit missionaries. For them, it was a calling that could cost them even their lives as martyrs. This calling was for them not some strategic career move, but a sacrifice. As Bolton notes, "These men came inspired by zeal for the saving of souls. Many of them were sons of distinguished families, who might have occupied positions of honor and distinction in Europe; most of them were men of liberal education; nearly all of them were zealous for the Faith, and wholly uninterested in private gain."[4]

Kino's first excursions took him to the Baja peninsula where he established the Misión San Bruno in 1683. It wasn't until 1687 that Kino began his work in Pimería Alta. He served in this massive region for twenty-four years until his death from fever in 1711. But Kino was more than just a Jesuit missionary. He impacted the region in many significant ways.

Once Father Kino arrived in the Pimería Alta, at the request of the natives, he quickly established the first mission in a river valley in the mountains of Sonora. Subsequently Kino traveled across northern Mexico, and to present day California and Arizona. He followed ancient trading routes established millennia prior by the natives. These trails were later expanded into roads. His many expeditions on horseback covered over 50,000 square miles (130,000 km^2), during which he mapped an area 200 miles (320 km) long and 250 miles (400 km) wide. Kino was

---

[4] *The Padre on Horseback*, 12.

important in the economic growth of the area, working with the already agricultural indigenous native peoples and introducing them to European seeds, fruits, herbs and grains. He also taught them to raise cattle, sheep and goats. Kino's initial mission herd of twenty cattle imported to Pimería Alta grew during this period to 70,000.[5]

Kino was a true scholar and entrepreneur. He brought over farming techniques and seeds that greatly aided the people. He also authored books on religion, astronomy, and cartography. What a legacy and impact he left!

Reading about Kino's story in light of today's emphasis on training church planters, there seems to be something that we have lost. With our inordinate amount of emphasis on preaching, creating and curating Sunday gatherings, leadership development, and so on, I wonder if we're short-changing the communities and the people that we seek to impact with the gospel. Could or should we be doing more than starting worship gatherings and doing evangelism?

Church Planting + Economic Development

For the sake of brevity, I have only recounted a few key points from the exemplary life of Father Kino. There is so much more to tell that space

---

[5] Wikimedia, LLC, "Eusebio Kino", para. 7. Cited from Bolton, Herbert Eugene. *The Padre on Horseback. a Sketch of Eusebio Francisco Kino S. J. Apostle to the Pimas*. Sonora Press.

does not permit. But I believe I've given you enough to make my point. Let's say we were to take how we do church planting today in North America and apply it to Kino's life, methods, and strategies. Would we even have remembered him? Would there be anything worthy of documenting at all?

You see, the goal of church planting today is first and foremost to start new churches and hopefully to see exponential growth. The legacy that most church planters long to leave is large churches with large numbers of souls saved. But are we too limited in our scope? What if Kino had had that same end goal?

Kino did indeed have a passion for lost souls. "Nothing gave Father Kino such true pleasure as some sign that an Indian was becoming interested in the Faith."[6] But what if? What if Kino had never introduced new crops and farming techniques? What if he had never expanded his herd of cattle that allowed the villages to prosper economically? "And it must not be supposed that he did this for private gain, for he did not own a single animal. It was to furnish a food supply for the Indians of the missions established and to be established, and to give these missions a basis of economic prosperity and independence."[7]

We could say that Kino extended both saving grace and common grace to the Pimas. He not

---

[6] *The Padre on Horseback*, 34.
[7] Ibid., 59.

only sought to evangelize the Pimas (saving grace), but he manifested a gospel that led to their flourishing socially and economically (common grace). Therein lies the rub in church planting today in North America. Are we thinking and acting like missionaries or are we merely clergy leading religious services?

I see it all the time. New church planters move to a city in an attempt to launch worship services. The bulk of their time and effort goes toward starting these gatherings. That is not to say that the gathered church, the teaching of God's word, and worshipping through song are unimportant. But the point I want to make is that if we moved to a foreign country, we'd engage in missionary activities. Why not here?

Obviously, Kino truly was an cross-cultural missionary. He not only had to learn new languages, but also new customs and cultures, and immerse himself in the unique setting of the Sonoran Desert. For whatever reason, it seems easier to make the switch into "missionary mode" when we're far from home and in foreign settings than when we're in a North American setting. The challenge looms as to whether we're to think and act like this at *home*.

This is the tension I hope to carry throughout this book. While I will continually poke and prod at these topics and ideas, I will not do so out of some deep-seated frustration towards the church. In fact, I love church planters. I have been a church planter. My life revolves around church planting. Most of my friends are church planters. My calendar is filled with having coffee with church planters and training them. I want to move this conversation forward from a positive, proactive perspective rather than one that is critical and negative.

My intention is to expand and challenge our collective thinking in order to burrow deeper into a missionary ethos as church planters. My hope is that we will see ourselves more as church-planting missionaries than as pastors starting worship services. That "missionary" label then becomes key. It frees us up. It gives us permission to be truly innovative and entrepreneurial. Not "innovative" in the sense of tweaking worship gatherings to make them more appealing, but "entrepreneurial" in the sense of a Father Kino. To seek to not only proclaim the gospel, but to live it out in radically culture-altering ways that will leave an impact hundreds of years after we're gone. With all of this in mind, I needed to revisit the San Xavier del Bac Mission.

The White Dove of the Desert

Visiting Tucson and the Sonoran Desert in the summer is normally a recipe for disaster. Having been away for nearly a decade, I've lost my tolerance for the heat. On June 30th, I landed at the airport in Tucson. Its air-conditioning didn't prepare me for the wave of hot air that enveloped me as I stepped outside to pick up my rental car. But it didn't matter. Because I was on a mission. To see a mission.

The drive from the airport to San Xavier is relatively short, and before long I was already exiting Interstate 19 to head towards the mission. This stretch of the Sonoran Desert is somewhat harsh. The lushness found in such places as the foothills of the Santa Catalinas is instead replaced by sparse terrain punctuated by saguaros and creosote. However, in the midst of it all stands the White Dove of the Desert—the San Xavier del Bac Mission.

Founded by Kino in 1692, the original structure is gone. Bits and pieces were used to build the current mission which was built between 1783 and 1797. In light of the long and rich history of Arizona—including human occupation dating back to Clovis Man in 13,000 BC and an unearthed mammoth kill site, not to mention its many Pre-Columbian communities before the arrival of Europeans in 1539—Kino's presence in southern Arizona can feel incredibly recent. But in terms of European settlement across the continent it is significant.

Pulling up to the parking lot in front of the mission, one is struck immediately with why it has earned the nickname "The White Dove of the Desert." The white adobe walls illuminate the structure like a massive spotlight, as if it is radiating its own light source. Depending on where you're at in the area, you can see San Xavier for miles. Glowing. Illuminating. A beacon of hope?

Revisiting an Old Friend

I made my way straight to the sanctuary. Even though the summer temperatures outside were scorching, it was comfortable upon entering. I found an empty pew in the back and slid in. My senses were alive and overloaded. The air was thick with the scent of candles from the hundreds that were burning up front near the altar. The decor itself is a visual masterpiece of colorful and intricate murals, statues, and designs. It has a gaudy kind of feel, but at the same time it fits. It is easy for Protestants to be dismissive of ornate Catholic buildings or icons, but in reality, they are simply telling a story visually. In some ways, this can be even more profound than words can express.

Sitting there on the hard, wooden pew, I was reminded that this is not simply some tourist stop but is still an active church. Many people, mainly from the Tohono O'odham San Xavier Indian Reservation, were there to worship and pray. If there was ever a building that truly felt like a sacred place, this was it.

I did have a *Nacho Libre* moment, though. If you remember from early on in the movie, Nacho, played by Jack Black, is sitting in the back of the church drawing a luchador in his sketchbook.

Obviously, he is not paying attention to the priest who is leading Mass. As he colors in his book, he suddenly becomes aware of a presence hovering over him and watching. He looks up to see a statue of a late saint on the wall solemnly gazing down. Nacho abruptly shuts his sketchbook and begins to pay attention.

Maybe that was why I was there that day at San Xavier. To visit this sacred place, to feel the presence of Someone looking down on me to utter a word (or words) of confirmation or encouragement for the new direction in life and ministry on which I was about ready to embark. Along with that, I had this urge to reconnect with the story and life of Father Eusebio Kino. I'm not a hundred percent sure what we'd say today about his contextualization efforts, but I have to applaud him for trying. Besides, since the start of the church in the first century, I'd venture to say that we continuously wrestle with contextualization. How far is too far? How far is not enough? When do we cross the line into syncretism? When do we become so rigid that we refuse to enculturate the church and the gospel into the fluidity of culture?

This was why I wanted to visit Kino, or at least the legacy he left. Regardless of our thoughts about the work of the Jesuits and Franciscans throughout the Southwest, and Central and South America, there is one thing we cannot deny. They left a lasting legacy. Again, not every one of them lived a life which honored God, but I wanted to know why these bold pioneers are still revered and remembered today for their work centuries ago. What can we learn? Also, far from being dubbed "Christendom," what if we began to think of North America in terms of a mission field.

2

SOCIAL ENTREPRENEURIALISM + CHURCH PLANTING

++++++++++++++

It seems as if today everyone is an entrepreneur. Many social media profiles flaunt the self-proclaimed title "entrepreneur." But is it really that easy? I've always preferred to stay away from titles and such. Former British Prime Minister Margaret Thatcher once quipped, "Power is like being a lady ... if you have to tell people you are, you aren't." Sometimes I wonder: If you have to tell people you are an entrepreneur, are you really?

I think we need to hit the pause button simply to point out that this trend is nothing new. Yes, the medium has changed and because of social media and technology we're seeing more and more overnight sensations, millionaires, and celebrities. However, long before we began exchanging currency, people were starting businesses. They may have been exchanging manual labor for a place to stay, or beets and carrots for handiwork, but in many ways, entrepreneurialism has always been a basic human practice.

Urban Economics

For the past several years, I've taught an upper division college course called History of the American City. There are many layers to studying and understanding history. We repeatedly look at the developing economies throughout American history because they have played an enormous role in shaping cities. Technological development plus industrial growth created a unique phenomenon initially known only to American cities—the *downtown*.

Robert Fogelson notes in his book *Downtown: Its Rise and Fall, 1880-1950*, "Although hard to define, downtown was easy to locate. It was the destination of the street railways, which were still pulled by horses in the 1880s, the elevated railways, which ran above the streets of New York, and the local ferries, which carried millions a year in a handful of cities."[1] This was all a reflection of an economic transition from an artisan economy to an industrial economy.

In each era, entrepreneurs were launching businesses, whether it was a blacksmith shop in Boston in the late 1700s, or industrial giants like Carnegie or Rockefeller, or today's tech giants like Steve Jobs, Bill Gates, Mark Zuckerberg, or Elon Musk. Different economic eras and technology, but the same impulse.

Into this world steps a church planter. In many ways, since the beginning of the church as recorded in Acts, church planters or missionaries have been its entrepreneurs. Starting churches from scratch in new locations is a very creative

---

[1] Fogelson, *Downtown*, 13.

and entrepreneurial endeavor. In the same way that business entrepreneurs have changed their approaches throughout history because of technological advances and changes in local and global economies, church planters also continue to adapt with the changing times. We saw this in the life of Father Kino. If we dropped Kino into the 21st century, rather than establishing himself as a cattle baron he might have been a software developer or media maven.

Making a Living

Another layer of the conversation we need to address is how pastors, missionaries, or church planters make a living. In recent modern (and Western) history, it was understood that the career trajectory of someone in "full-time" ministry was to begin with Bible college and/or seminary. Upon graduation, they would transition into a full-time ministry position in the church or be sent as a missionary. Many still operate under this framework. However, what many of us observe is that, a) this is becoming less and less the case, b) more often than not this is not the reality for ethnic minority churches where bi-vocationalism is an everyday reality, and c) this is not how the church in the rest of the world operates. Meaning, it would appear that oftentimes to be a pastor means to be bi-vocational.

If that's the case, then what does a church planter, missionary, or pastor do to earn a living or supplement their income? For those who were on the career trajectory of Bible college and seminary, it means that the training and academic focus has been so ministry-oriented that it's not always easily translatable into occupations outside of ministry. I discovered this when I first became a church planter.

After college, my wife and I moved to Phoenix to attend seminary. It was during that time that I went on staff at a church as a youth pastor. Five years later, after having been a youth pastor in two churches, I transitioned into church planting in Tucson. While we had good funding, it wasn't enough to meet our financial needs as a growing family (we had just had Baby #3). As a result, I had to find a "real" job outside of ministry. The problem was that all of my education and work experience after college had been in the local church. What was I to do?

While I feel like I have a creative bent to me, I was nowhere near thinking about doing anything entrepreneurial. I was full-on in the ministry mindset, and when it came to jobs my goal was to find the best one I could stomach that would allow me to do what I really love—being in full-time ministry. I applied and sent my resume out to a number of businesses. After a month, I received a call to interview for the position of a hiking and mountain biking guide at a local destination spa.

I ended up getting that job. I worked at it over a five-year stretch, at times one or two mornings a week and at other times full-time. Towards the end, while I was working on my DMin, I felt I had had enough of bi-vocationalism and was ready for an exit. But probably like many of you, in the years that followed I had and still have other jobs on the side. Apart from serving as an interim pastor, most of my "side jobs" have taken the form of city cycling guide, adjunct professor, research coordinator for an urban sustainability project at a public university, graphic designer, author, and more.

Church Planting and the Artisan Economy

My life was significantly influenced when I came across the book *Brew to Bikes: Portland's Artisan Economy* written by Charles Heying. Shortly after arriving in Portland, I was losing my interest in ministry as an occupation, and I began a PhD in urban studies at Portland State University. It was there that I encountered Heying, who is a professor at Portland State, and his book. The big take-away for me was that many businesses in Portland's artisan / maker economy have sprung up with little to no start-up costs or investment. Many of our beloved local businesses, from coffee roasters to breweries to clothing lines and more, began with nothing more than a deep sense of conviction ("I *must* do this").

So my thought was, *why not me?* I started a publishing company more by accident than by any well-thought-out business plan. Across the street at our neighborhood McDonalds sipping bad $1 coffee, I would sit at my laptop writing, thinking, planning, designing, recruiting, and doing my best with very limited know-how to figure out how to grow this fledgling company. It was a fun time and I learned a lot. However, after three years, I realized that, a) I had no desire to be the president or CEO of a publishing company long-term, and b) the company needed new leadership to take it to the next level. It was a joy and relief to sell it because I needed the break and it is now in much more capable hands.

Towards the end, there was a six month overlap when I launched a coffee roasting company. Again, as with the publishing company, it was almost more by accident than by any grand scheme of mine. And this time, my life was surrounded by urban-focused ministry and academia. It was as though I needed a mental and emotional break. Not only that, but a physical break to actually *do* something other than sit in front of a computer screen. That's when roasting coffee became an outlet for me. Something physical, something tangible—the smell of coffee roasting, the heat from the roaster, the sound of beans hitting the first crack, and more.

It was during this time that I read *The Padre on Horseback* and began noticing a change in my heart. Up to that point, I had naively looked at ministry as something that needed to be done full-time, while any sense of bi-vocationalism was more or less a distraction, something to tide people over until the ministry could afford to pay a full-time salary. But through reading the book, and in light of my own experiences with my roasting company, I was attentive to the joy and thrills of this life "outside" of ministry. Not only that, but I was connecting with more and more people in ways I didn't or couldn't before, just like when I was a mountain biking guide.

Kino's life was a jolt to awaken me to the fact that as pastors, church planters, or missionaries, there is *so much more* we can be about than simply "religious duties." In other words, rather than looking at the two silos of "ministry" versus "secular work," why not see everything as sacred? Not only that, but they can be combined and we can leverage one for the other for the betterment of the community we're seeking to live in and proclaim the gospel to. That puts us on a collision course with social entrepreneurship.

Social Entrepreneurship

Much has been written about this topic of late, from micro-finance to TOM's Shoes and more. It is certainly wide-ranging and far-reaching. What is social entrepreneurship? In a nutshell, it is about pursuing an innovative idea to solve a community problem. It is the combination, if you will, of business and social justice. It is leveraging your business for the betterment of the community or for addressing some specific problem.

While there are myriad definitions out there, a quick perusal online reveals a lot of overlap and commonalities. Here are two for discussion's sake:

> What is a 'Social Entrepreneur'? A person who pursues an innovative idea with the potential to solve a community problem. These individuals are willing to take on the risk and effort to create positive changes in society through their initiatives.[2]

> Social entrepreneurship is the use of the techniques by start-up companies and other entrepreneurs to develop, fund and implement solutions to social, cultural, or environmental issues.[3]

Those definitions suffice for the context of this book. Again, we're talking about launching legitimate businesses that have the dual aim of: a) making money, and b) meeting a need in the community. The important thing to keep in mind is that this straddles the line between *both*. Making money and meeting community needs are not incompatible. One isn't more noble than the other. This is where the tension comes in.

Why does this matter? Looking once again at Father Kino's life and the brief snapshots we have

---

[2] Investopia, LLC, "Social Entrepreneur," para. 1.
[3] Wikimedia Foundation, Inc, "Social entrepreneurship," para. 1.

seen, one could easily label him a "social entrepreneur." I'm sure he would bristle under that label and insist that his only desire was to serve God and the Pimas. However, in practice one can make the case that this is certainly what he *did*. While the label "priest" did apply and was more or less his identity, it didn't keep him from leveraging business assets (cattle) for the betterment of the community.

I believe Father Kino's example also reveals the tension of this book or at least the idea that I'm putting forth. Much of this angst or inner turmoil may then be about identity and labels. Who are you? Who am I? Am I a minister? A church planter? A missionary? Or am I a business entrepreneur? If we choose one label over another, does that mean we can't do or be the other?

What this also reveals is the perceived restrictions that happen when we apply labels. Was the apostle Paul at odds with his calling as a missionary to the Gentiles when he simultaneously plied his trade as a tent-maker? In fact, he stated that he did this so as to not be a burden to the church. Was he at odds with his calling? Was he only partially living out God's plan for his life as a missionary? Or did in fact his trade *assist* him in his endeavors to bring the gospel to the Gentiles? I'm not at all attempting to shoehorn Paul into the social entrepreneur category. He might have been. We simply don't know.

This whole conversation about labels, titles, and identity may seem trivial, but it's a real issue. I know it is important for me and for many others who are in full-time ministry (however we define or quantify that). This has been part of my internal wrestling because, as I shared earlier, it gets to the heart of identity and ultimately calling. Those are both intensely personal.

Did I foresee when I came to faith in Christ and began my journey toward becoming a pastor/missionary, that along the way I'd be a hiking and mountain biking guide? A publisher? A coffee roaster? A professor? If I could have looked into the future, what would I have thought of my middle-aged self? If you're like me, then you've at least entertained those thoughts. Why? Because the bottom line is that we want to live a life in sync with the calling we sense that God has placed on us.

I realize that by letting you into my little world, I risk sounding foolish. But these are the exact kinds of conversations I've been having with my wife lately. I told her honestly that I often feel torn and pulled in three distinct directions: 1) ministry as an "occupation," 2) academia as a professor, and 3) business as a coffee roaster. Many days I feel these competing interests pulling me in different directions. Most of the time, my internal wrestling revolves around how to synchronize these three seemingly disparate pieces. I can't say that I've found a solution yet, and so I simply live with the tension.

Identity and Calling

For many of us, much of the tension revolves around this discussion of identity and calling. What do we sense God doing in our lives? How then do we more succinctly bring these worlds together to the point that there is no more inner conflict or tension?

As I looked at the current state of church planting through the lens of the life of Father Kino, it dawned on me how much we're missing out on in terms of the longer-term impact and influence we could be having on the communities we love and serve. This is not anything new—not a new paradigm, not a new program, or anything like that—but simply *another* way to engage in church planting that has a more (and I hate to use this word) *holistic* scope.

I understand that we're all wired uniquely and that there is no simple, cookie cutter approach to church planting. When local context is factored in, this conversation becomes that much more nuanced, contextual, and layered. What one person does in one setting does not apply in another setting, because while there are commonalities, each planter and each place are so different. No two church planters or missionaries are alike, and no two settings are alike, even when they're in different neighborhoods within the same city.

For nearly two years now, I've been working on and developing a church-planting and start-up incubator called Intrepid (hence the title of this book). To boil it down, it is an attempt to train, catalyze, and put into practice the motif of Father Kino. Not copy or emulate, but learn from, extract, and apply it to our current settings. Here are a couple observations from Kino's life that serve as a rudder for Intrepid.

First, he leveraged his background, interests, education, and training for the betterment of the community and people that he was serving. For him that meant his training and experience in farming, cartography, and the like. Those skills came to play a significant role in shaping his work among the Pima and left a lasting legacy.

Second, he went to an overlooked and off-the-beaten-path kind of place. In some ways, he was a pioneer church-planting missionary. He left the comforts of Europe and the life he could have lived to instead trek thousands of miles on horseback around the harsh, arid Sonoran Desert of southern Arizona and northern Mexico. It is challenging enough to live there today with all the modern conveniences, but one can only imagine how challenging it was to be a frontier priest in the hinterlands.

Identity, Calling, and Place

I bring up that second point with a lot of passion behind it. My last book, *Urban Hinterlands:*

Planting the Gospel in Uncool Places, focuses on this very subject. One of the most glaring observations I've had in fifteen years of involvement in church planting is that *most* of the time church planters opt to go to desirable and livable places. This could range from family-friendly suburbs with excellent schools to trendy urban neighborhoods that have gentrified. This is not a conversation about the rightness or wrongness of any of that, but a look instead at people like Kino who moved in the opposite direction.

Intrepid's mission is to partner with and mobilize local churches to plant new churches across North America in under-reached and off-the-beaten-path communities, particularly communities that have been in economic decline and are transitioning to revitalize their local economy (both urban and rural). It is to see churches planted where people come to Christ and the community is lifted up through new businesses, non-profits, job creation, and more.

One of Intrepid's goals is to establish a network of new church plants in such communities with the simultaneous goal of community and economic development through new business start-ups that seek the flourishing of these communities. That's it. Straightforward.

Geography influences how and where most churches are planted. When we think about international missions, there's a propensity and compulsion to go, to serve, and to give away our lives among the last and the least. Obviously, this is an oversimplification, but the point is that we really don't hesitate to think about giving our lives away in the slums *over there*.

Geography.

There is a declining emphasis on church planting in smaller communities outside of our growing urban centers, as resources are redirected towards cities. We find many first-ring suburbs to be the landing place for immigrants and those displaced from gentrification.

Geography.

So how we do change the narrative? How do we do here what we do over there?

Where Church Planters Tread

Change is sweeping across North America's cities. For the first time since the early 20th century, city centers are growing faster than their suburban counterparts. Along with this population inversion, we have seen a growing number of new churches and ministries launched in the urban core. In many cities, even in large ones like Chicago, typical church planters are opting to plant their lives and the gospel within the city limits rather than the suburbs.

It Is Really About Economics

One of the most prolific change agents in cities today is the local and global economy. As a post-industrial / post-manufacturing nation, our greatest economic output is now derived from the Creative Class (that is, the knowledge-based workforce). Not only is this socio-economic grouping altering the urban fabric, but the trickle-down effect is being felt far and wide, even outside major urban areas. Google, Facebook, and other high-tech companies continue to set up shop in smaller communities with databases and more. Small towns once dependent upon resource extraction (such as logging, fishing, or mining) have thrown their lot into capturing this mobile capital through tourism. For example, tourism brings $19 billion annually into the economy of British Columbia. In Oregon, bike-oriented tourism alone pumps $400 million a year into the state's economy.

The Rise of the "Other"

Small cities and other smaller communities are reinventing themselves to attract and retain not only these illusive and yet vital tourism dollars, but they are also wooing the migratory Creative Class. Prominent cities like Hood River, Oregon, Park City, Utah, and Whistler, British Columbia, are hotspots for livability, outdoor amenities, and an active lifestyle. Many other cities like Oakridge, Oregon, Leavenworth, Washington, and

Revelstoke, BC, are former logging communities that are being revitalized by their new focus on tourism, specifically mountain biking tourism, and have poured millions of dollars into building and expanding their trail systems. However, that is only the beginning, as the end goal is about bringing in new residents who are drawn to these amenity-rich communities.

The Intrepid Perspective

The idea behind Intrepid is to start a network / strategy that focuses on starting churches in neglected communities, whether in cities or in rural settings. However, this goes beyond merely church planting as we have come to define it in North America. Intrepid is viewed through the interpretive lens of international missions. In other words, we want to send missionaries into these communities who not only start churches, but who are also focused on economic and community development by becoming entrepreneurs who start small businesses as well as non-profits.

Church Planting + Community Development = Gospel Renewal

Our two-pronged approach to mission is to couple together church planting with community development. This is not anything new, nor a different strategy. But it defines both who we are as well as our approach to church planting. When we go into a community (or mobilize people and teams to go into communities), we want to see the gospel proclaimed and lived out, and new believers gathered together for worship, instruction, and modeling as part of the discipleship process. We also want to benefit and be an asset to the community—whether it be an urban neighborhood, a small city, or a small town—by starting new businesses or non-profits and even helping shape or improve the urban form or the environment of the city.

With all of that said, this only makes sense if we actually view North America as a mission field.

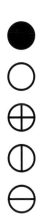

3

NORTH AMERICA
AS A NEW FRONTIER

+++++++++++++

When I was in college I continued to wrestle with this call to "missions." I wasn't sure what "missions" even meant. All I knew was that I had surrendered my life to Christ and was willing and able to go anywhere and do anything he wanted me to do. In conventional missions thinking, this would then entail planning for a life of living abroad. However, even then I was looking at how North America is a mission field. I began reflecting on growing up in small-town Iowa and all of the people I knew. *Most* were not followers of Christ. I recall in high school, even though I was not yet a Christian, only knowing a handful of people who identified with Christ. The small-town Midwest was and is a mission field.

While I was interested in a number of countries across the globe, I never actually left the homeland. In fact, even though during a missions conference in college I surrendered again to missions, committing to go anywhere and do anything that the Lord would have for me, I never left. I never "went" to the mission field. You see, I live *on* and *in* the mission field—this new but old frontier called North America.

At first glance it may sound like I was and am a Jonah who's running from the Lord. Staying instead of going. My friend Alan Briggs addresses this very dichotomy in a book he wrote called *Staying is the New Going.* He writes,

> For a long time now mission has been framed as a far-off endeavor, a trip requiring a passport, a plane ticket, and a lot of packing. But God's mission is active everywhere, which means God's mission is active among your family, friends, and community. For God's work to become tangible, it must first become local, invading our everyday thinking and the places we inhabit.[1]

Since I didn't become a Christian until after high school, I believe it spared me from thinking about the standard geographic dichotomy between "missions" (international) and "ministry" (domestic). To me, everywhere was the mission field. In college, I began to specifically pray, "Lord, if you want me to stay in North America, please let me go to the darkest places in need of the gospel." So the Lord led us to Tucson, Arizona.

The Old Pueblo

If you were to read my previous books, one theme that resurfaces repeatedly is a place. Tucson. It is a gritty and sprawling Southwest desert city that has captured and still captures my heart. While the surrounding desert is stunningly beautiful, the city itself looks like it was

---

[1] Briggs, *Staying is the New Going*, 6.

haphazardly thrown together by an eight-year-old. However, what initially repulsed me about Tucson soon became endearing.

Many who move to Tucson for ministry reasons admit that there is a certain spiritual darkness hovering over the city that is almost tangible. I have never lived in another city where there was this sense of heaviness. But I could sense it, feel it, and it was certainly noticeable. At times, it was eerie. It drove me to pray all the more for the people and for our church-planting efforts.

As a new church planter in the city, I met with a number of pastors to seek their wisdom about church planting as well as make connections and friends. I was encouraged by all of the Kingdom-minded leaders there who welcomed us in. One conversation in particular stood out. I met with a pastor of one of the largest churches in the city. Jerry did a masterful job of weaving together for me the spiritual background and realities of Tucson. He then proceeded to tell me about the spiritual warfare that was a regular reality in their church body. In fact, they had a department dedicated to it. From dealing with self-proclaimed witches in their worship services to exorcisms and other "paranormal" phenomena, I listened intently to learn exactly what kind of city I had just moved to. By the way, Jerry was on staff at a large conservative Southern Baptist church.

During our church-planting endeavors and work in the city, we saw and personally experienced some hair-raising situations that left an indelible mark on our lives. There are some events that we've not even told our boys about, because they were just toddlers at the time. Needless to say, the prayer I had uttered in college and my commitment before the Lord was being tested and lived out. Tucson was and is a very spiritually dark place.

Why am I telling you this? Not to sensationalize anything, but to begin challenging you to adjust your thinking and realize that here in North America, we truly are living in a mission field. Why is that admission even pertinent? I am convinced that if that thought would somehow "click" with you, it would begin to *change everything* in how we think about church planting across the US and Canada. Why?

Here vs. There

You see, when we relocate abroad to be missionaries, it changes the rules of engagement and strategy. We spend an inordinate amount of time looking to become an "insider" or at least become fluent in the local language and culture. We look for persons of peace. We hammer through contextualization not only in how we teach and proclaim the gospel, but in how we demonstrate the gospel. We exegete our cities and communities. We put on our contextualization goggles again when it comes to gathering new believers together for instruction, discipleship, worship, and prayer. We think and talk about movements and exponential, multiplicative growth. And there is a myriad of other missionary skills that we embrace and live out.

But, when it comes to church planting in North America, we jettison most of these things and immediately begin planning for "launch Sunday," focusing all our efforts on making a trendy and entertaining worship gathering. Even when confronted with these truths and this dichotomy, church planters are quick to point out that *here* we simply do church like we've always done in the West. Church planters seem like they can't wait until they get an office and move in with their books so they can spend fifteen hours a week studying and writing their sermons. Supposedly most of the rest of their time is then dedicated to the Sunday gathering—pushing social media, coordinating graphic design and other media, picking out the song list (and tweeting about it), and so on.

That was my story. And if you're planting a North American church, I suspect that is your story as well.

In the process of church planting, whether we're "pre-launch" or "post-launch," this is how we think. I don't remember anything other than the inordinate amount of work and planning that went into "launching big," even though our launch more or less resembled a toy rocket falling off the launch pad. All our efforts were focused on growing our core group, multiplying community groups, marketing, pre-launch events, and the like. Then, once we started with weekly gatherings, all attention was directed towards growing that gathering numerically.

I found out later, or maybe I should say I realized later, that I wasn't good at any of that. I'm not that good at marketing and hyping a new church plant. I hate self-promotion. I'm simply not the kind of leader who can passionately stand before crowds and woo them into getting onboard to head in a certain direction.

Maybe that's the crux of the matter. Maybe if I *was* talented in those areas I wouldn't be writing this book. Instead I'd be into writing books about growing your church, turning crowds into disciples, leadership principles, bold vision, and the like. Instead, I write about niche topics such as church planting in obscure places, walkability and bikeability, urban cycling, gentrification, and other topics in which the church-planting mainstream is seemingly not interested.

The Unwritten Rules of Church Planting

Even as an active church planter, I was wrestling with this dichotomy of church planting versus missions. I was *supposed* to do church planting in a certain way. I am still not sure who wrote this unwritten rule book, but the book must exist because every church plant is judged by it. It's kind of like the unwritten rules in baseball ... Don't talk about a no-hitter if the pitcher has one going into the seventh inning, don't excessively celebrate when you hit a home run but fist pump all you want when you strike out a batter, and other absurdities.

Am I being harsh? Yes. Why? Because if we sent a missionary overseas, we would chastise them if they planted a church in this way in, say, Paris or Copenhagen or Tokyo or Singapore. So what's behind the disconnect?

The dichotomy.

Until we who are US- or Canada-based missionaries are truly ready to think and act differently, we'll continue on the same old trajectory. Big, attractive gatherings for the mostly-convinced in which the majority of the church, apart from its leaders, are passive spectators. But if we were to actually view our home turf as a mission field, it would begin to change everything.

The Changing Landscape of North American Pioneer Missions

Since I'm committed to North American missions and living in places where the spiritual needs are great, I have a keen interest in deciphering where these "frontier" places truly are. The challenge is that they are a moving target that continues to shift and evolve. In fact, we're in the midst of a significant momentum change right now.

In the early 2000s, I served as a Church Planting Strategist in Tucson. It was an exhilarating time of ministry. With the whole metropolitan area before me, my role was to catalyze new churches particularly in those parts of the city and among people where there was the greatest spiritual need. I came to the task pretty green, but I jumped in wholeheartedly.

A few years into the role, I began noticing a trend. Most church planters I talked with, whether they were visiting the city while exploring a call to plant a church, or actually coming and planting, opted to look into starting churches in the suburbs. Particularly in new master-planned communities being built from scratch. From a missions perspective, this was to some degree spot-on. Some of these brand-new communities had gone from zero to 10,000 to 20,000 people in only a handful of years. It was imperative to plant churches there and in similar communities.

This was the heyday of the housing boom that acutely impacted Arizona and other Sunbelt states. I scoured the internet tracking these changes and the incoming new communities. Some were small, consisting of only a few hundred homes, while others were projected to have 30,000 people once they were built out. We couldn't plant churches fast enough to keep up with the new subdivisions.

However, in all this excitement, which impacted how I recruited church planters and the flurry of activity that went along with that, I had missed something. Something pretty significant. It hit me suddenly one morning while sitting and thinking in a coffee shop just outside of downtown Tucson: *We were not planting churches in the city.* I looked at all of the new churches and all of the church planters I was in conversation with, and *most* were opting for the suburbs. I had completely overlooked the urban core.

To be fair, as I mentioned earlier, the city's explosive growth in these new master-planned communities meant that we needed to plant a lot of churches in a hurry simply to try and keep up with the population growth. However, at the same time, it hit me that *no one* was planting in the city—in the urban core, downtown. At that time, I was connected with the whole church-planting scene and I realized that no one else was planting in the city either.

That realization sent me on a personal quest that altered the entire trajectory of my academic and ministry life. Why weren't we planting in the city center? I researched other large cities throughout the West and the same storyline unfolded in city after city. But that was over ten years ago now. The tide has changed—and *rapidly*.

Case in point. After a six-year absence, I visited Tucson for the first time since moving away in 2008. One of the shifts I immediately noticed upon connecting with church planters is that there is now a wave of new church start-ups in the urban core. Over just a few years, I had watched the geographic emphasis in church planting shift radically from suburban fringe to urban core. What was only a trickle in Tucson in 2014 was already a torrent in other cities, especially in cool places like Portland.

I have talked with other denominational leaders who head up church planting in their cities and I have listened as they share about all the years they spent praying for new churches to be started downtown and in the urban cores. Like Tucson, most new churches had been started in the suburban or exurban fringes. But the tide has shifted. Church planters tend to follow migration patterns in their city. And right now, we're in the midst of an explosive population in-migration back to the heart of the city.

There is a myriad of reasons why Americans have "rediscovered" their downtowns, but the main two are an economic shift to a knowledge-based or creative economy (and away from manufacturing), and a thirst for an urban existence. People have begun flocking to the city centers. And like church planters did when they followed the population wave to the fringes, now they are following the people back to the city center.

Whereas it was an anomaly two decades ago in Portland to plant a church in the inner city, it's now the standard. Wave after wave of new church planters are moving into the urban core, oftentimes several to the same neighborhood. I regularly meet up with prospective church planters just as I did while I was in Tucson. But now the storyline has completely flipped with *most* new church planters opting not only for the city, but for the urban core.

A Shift

So why mention this? Because I feel like I am in the midst of a transition myself in terms of the geography of mission, or church planting, in North America. For the past decade, I was a "city guy." Everything I read, wrote, researched, and taught on was about how and why church planting in the city was essential. You see, for me it was a pioneer missionary endeavor. If very little emphasis was being given to planting there, I was all in. And I was.

I read and devoured information about the city. I studied urban and transportation planning in school. I devoted much time and attention to tracking urban economics and how we move around the city. But as time went on, I began to notice something changing in my heart.

At first, I was terrified and thought I was battling depression or something. I was losing interest in the city. It really started to set in as I watched church planter after church planter move into the heart of the city. What initially drew me to the city was that there was little emphasis on planting there; but once the tide began turning, my internal angst began growing. This was worrisome for me, especially since I was in the midst of teaching at several universities on the city, urban church planting, understanding cities, economics, urban mobility, community development, and a theology of the city.

And then it finally clicked for me. God has wired me for "pioneer" endeavors. While the heart of the city had once been that setting for me, I now found myself searching for a new frontier. Then my question became: Where is the new frontier for missions and church planting in North America?

Now before I move down this path any farther, I need to press the pause button. Not all cities are the same, and trends are felt more acutely in some cities than in others. Have things changed? Yes, for sure. However, in places like Tucson the shift has reached nowhere near the saturation levels of urban cores like Portland. Not even in the same galaxy. Tucson needs more waves of church planters willing to move into the heart of the city and into the lower-income neighborhoods and barrios that make up its urban core.

So where then is this new frontier?

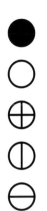

4

THE NEW FRONTIER

+++++++++++++++

I did not start out intentionally thinking about the "new frontier" in North American missions, but in retrospect I did begin moving in that direction. It happened more out of personal angst and frustration than some proactive search. My previous book, *Urban Hinterlands*, marked a decisive shift for me. This shift was and is geographic. Not necessarily away from the city but questioning why we tend to plant churches in North America mostly in attractive cities and trendy neighborhoods. This tendency explains why for many years we didn't really plant churches in Tucson's urban core—it wasn't that cool or attractive.

The whole trajectory of *Urban Hinterlands* was about exploring livability and ultimately what it would mean to plant churches in uncool cites and lackluster neighborhoods. Since then, as I have looked at these kinds of places and communities, it has begun to dawn on me that once again (at least for me) the frontier of North American missions has shifted.

The ongoing saturation of the urban core with new churches reflects a necessary course correction for having overemphasized for decades suburban church planting. But now the pendulum is swinging yet again. It is time to begin addressing *what's next* for North American church planting. To me, that new frontier is not only those uncool and undesirable cities and neighborhoods, but also those smaller communities located in the in-between places of our major metro areas. As well, recent economic changes mean that many communities that were traditionally dependent upon resource extraction (e.g., logging, mining, fishing, etc.) are now seeking to reinvent themselves to attract and retain not only tourism dollars, but also their share of the elusive and migratory creative class. You see, this conversation about creative-class theory is not only reshaping the urban context but has far-reaching ramifications and applications for small communities across the continent as well. Towns and small cities that we had once written off are on the rise.

Explorers and Pioneers

As I mentioned, I recently finished reading *The Padre on Horseback* which is a summary of the life and missionary journeys of Jesuit missionary Father Eusebio Kino, who planted a slew of missions in northern Mexico and southern Arizona over three hundred years ago. I then began reading *A Land So Strange: The Epic Journey of Cabeza de Vaca* by Andrés Reséndez. The back cover reads, "In 1528, a mission set out from Spain to colonize Florida. But the expedition went horribly wrong: Delayed by a hurricane, knocked off course by a colossal error of navigation, and ultimately doomed by a disastrous decision to separate the men from their ships, the mission quickly became a desperate journey of survival." While de Vaca was not a missionary (he was a royal treasurer), it seems that God used him mightily across the southwest in miraculous healings among the indigenous population.

Both of these books capture well for me the passion and sacrifice that missionaries have given since the birth of the church in Acts. Sure, I could've picked up other memoirs of more contemporary Protestant missionaries, but something intrigues me about the role of these men of God in the Southwest. I am also drawn to new ventures, new places to explore, and new experiences. In fact, I thrive on it. For that reason, I am drawn to the historic accounts of these missionaries and explorers coming to the "New World" in hopes of sharing the gospel.

I am not blind to the fact that this was done in conjunction with Spanish military conquest and colonial exploitation. While there are numerous accounts of Jesuits protecting indigenous peoples from enslavement, the brutal conditions of forced labor, and so on, it was all under the umbrella of the King of Spain and imperial expansion.[1]

However, what draws me to the stories of these missionaries is their pioneer ethos. They

---

[1] A good summary of this can be found in *A Short Account of the Destruction of the Indies* by 16th century Dominican priest Bartolome de las Casas.

explored, they mapped, they charted, they encountered new peoples and cultures, they learned new languages, and they sacrificed much. Many came from privileged families, and they could have enjoyed lives of ease, but instead they jettisoned it all. I like that. I get that. I want that.

While living in Tucson, I spent a great amount of time simply exploring. I would load up my family in our gas-guzzling Chevy Suburban and head out. Our explorations covered the whole gamut—from high-elevation alpine meadows to uncovering 600-year-old Hohokam village ruins to hiking along the San Pedro River to trekking through canyons and so much more. That hunger and thirst for exploration never stopped.

Our adventures took us off the beaten path through dusty mining towns that punctuate the desert with names like Globe and Clifton and Superior. Honestly, every time we drove through them, I would inwardly cringe. Who would want to live *there*? What kind of life would people have in such places?

I felt like Álvar Núñez Cabeza de Vaca, the marooned sixteenth-century Spaniard who escaped imprisonment and trekked across the American Southwest with several companions in the early 1500s. Historian Andrés Reséndez recounts, "Cabeza de Vaca and his companions were the first outsiders to have lived in the immense territories north of Mexico. Their accounts give us the rarest glimpses into precontact North America. These pioneers were able to see the continent before any other outsiders, prior to European contact."[2]

While in Arizona, I explored, I observed, and I made mental notes along the way during each of our journeys, thinking of the life and cultural differences between Sonoita and Sedona, Bisbee and Flagstaff, Prescott and Pinetop, and more. Since my role at that time was as a Church Planting Strategist, I would even begin imaging what it would take to plant churches in such places, whether it be a dusty and declining mining town or a hotspot like Sedona. It was akin to pioneer missions.

I understand the potential volatility and ethnocentrism surrounding the term "pioneer." You see, when we talk about pioneers, we do so usually from the perspective of a dominant white culture. But that does not diminish the reality of Native Americans who had been living there for thousands of years before European pioneers arrived. Likewise, in urban studies or urban ministry, we talk about pioneer gentrifiers, as if they are some noble lot going where no one has gone before. That also is dismissive of the people, mostly minorities, living in these neighborhoods that we had once written off. And yet I affirm this notion of the pioneer, because it speaks to what is new from the perspective of the person (or persons) who are doing the exploring.

---

[2] Resendez, *A Land So Strange*, 8.

The Rise and Fall of Communities

As I explored the desert throughout Arizona and New Mexico, I watched similar storylines emerge in different communities. "Boom to Bust" would be a common descriptor for many of these small cities and towns. For example, for a short time, Bisbee, Arizona, was the largest city between St. Louis and San Francisco. It was founded in 1880 as a copper, gold, and silver mining town. In the mid-twentieth century, with the decline in mining and numerous nearby mines closing, the population plummeted. The loss in jobs and population meant that the local economy was significantly impacted.

However, things began to turn around in the 1990s. With a growing focus on tourism and the attractiveness of this quirky place, people began to move there and amenities such as coffee shops and a live theater opened up. Because its downtown was built before the automobile, it is compact and walkable. Add to that the numerous Victorian-era homes and other architectural styles, such as art deco, and people realized that the "bones" of the city were worth preserving and restoring.

Today, Bisbee is a great story of a community that has transitioned from resource extraction to capturing the elusive tourism dollars and reinvestment. This same story is being replayed throughout the West. Even then, "success story" is hardly a good descriptor since the community still struggles economically. However, it'd be just another Arizona ghost town if it hadn't moved towards tourism.

Communities in Transition

The storyline is the same for logging towns here in the Pacific Northwest. Just as mines in the Southwest shut down and devastated local economies and livelihoods, the same happened in towns that saw their logging mills and operations cease. Economically and socially, things began spiraling out of control. Yet there are now numerous communities throughout Oregon on this continuum of reinventing themselves and reinvesting in a future apart from resource extraction.

Hood River to the east of Portland has transitioned from being a sleepy little town on the Columbia River to now being an outdoor adventure hotspot on par with such places as Telluride, Colorado, and Park City, Utah. Real estate in this town of 7,000 people is more expensive than in Portland. I recently read an article in the *Planetizen* newspaper about gentrification in unlikely places like Hood River. Thomas Sigler, in his article, "Is There Such a Thing as 'Rural' Gentrification?" notes:

> Rural gentrification heralds the placelessness and 'footloose' nature of work in the 21st Century. Drawn by preexisting cultural, geographic, and/or

historic assets, a small but significant
professional cohort has traded the bustle
of Metropolitan America for Smalltown,
USA. In the process, a smattering of
bucolic college towns, action sports
meccas, and colonial-era hamlets have
developed into economically and culturally
vibrant micropolises, thanks largely to the
endless possibilities afforded by e-
commerce and telecommuting.[3]

When we look at population dispersion across
the country, one of the common themes is that
there is always an ebb and flow. Cities that we
once called "great" have fallen from their lofty
perch.

As I mentioned, Bisbee was once the largest
city between St. Louis and San Francisco. Now it's
just a small town. In the 1920s Cleveland was not
only the fifth largest city in the U.S., but also a key
manufacturing center. However, in the 1960s the
economy slowed and people began fleeing to the
suburbs. In the 70s the city defaulted on its
federal loans.

The tide rises and falls on communities,
neighborhoods, and cities. Now this doesn't mean
that these once-important places ceased to exist.
Despite massive population loss, for example,
Detroit is still significant in many ways. But the
point is that we are still a migratory people, which
means cities will continue to rise and fall in

---

[3] Sigler, "Is There Such Thing as 'Rural' Gentrification?" para. 6.

prominence. Missiologically-speaking, then, this underscores the importance of ongoing cultural exegesis as we track trends and movements. Not only of people, but of capital and culture.

This brief history lesson reveals that "pioneer missions" or the "new frontier" is indeed a moving target. While cities will continue to play a central role in mission (and rightly so), we also need to be cognizant of the changes taking place around us that effect where we should invest time and personnel in mission endeavors.

The ideas in this book have been swirling around in my mind over the past couple of years. On weekends I sometimes load up my mountain bike and venture out into the wilderness to ride. Most of the good trails around Portland require an hour-plus drive to reach. That usually entails driving through small towns, such as Hood River or Oakridge, that are trying to reinvent themselves. Every time I drive through such a community, as I did in Arizona, I mentally map it and make notes.

Revitalizing Rural Economies

As a mountain biker, I regularly read magazines dedicated to this sport and the culture surrounding it. I have come across several articles related to Oakridge's attempt to transition economically from being a logging community to going all-in on mountain-biking tourism. In the last edition of *Freehub Magazine*, a group of editors, photographers, and riders headed up to Northern British Columbia to ride and document what is taking place in several communities that are moving away from dependence on resource extraction to tourism. Matt Cole writes:

> An entire ecosystem of northern communities is now staking a claim at the sport [mountain biking], quietly joining the ranks of the best riding in the province. Since the end of the gold rush, Northern BC has been subject to the economic booms and busts of logging and mining-- which, in recent years, have mostly been bust. In 2013, the Tourism Industry Association BC reports $13.9 billion in revenues. Compare that to the $15.7 for forestry and the $1.39 billion for mining, and recreational amenities like trails start to look like promising alternatives--and possible incentives to prompt the next big migration north.[4]

All across the continent, these smaller communities are reinventing themselves and reinvesting in tourism as well as amenities to secure a better future for successive generations. In our inordinate focus on cities, I wonder who is looking at these kinds of communities for church planting endeavors. This is why I'm drawn to the exploratory ethos of Kino and de Vaca. I believe we need to rekindle that ethos for today. Our

---

[4] Cole, "On Hell of a Party," 64.

advantage over these missionaries is that we don't have to travel across the ocean to live this out. We may simply have to relocate to places like Oakridge, Oregon, or Globe, Arizona, or even into aging first-ring suburbs that are the catch basins for the migrating urban poor.

The new frontier in North American missions continues to shift—from suburban to urban, and now from urban to first-ring lower income suburbs which are increasingly comprised of minorities, as well as smaller cities and towns. Let's tease out some of these thoughts and ideas. Again, I love cities. The larger and more diverse the better. I enjoy living an urban lifestyle in a mixed-use building in the city center with my bike and scooter. But the new frontier continues to shift.

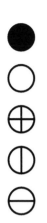

5

CHURCH PLANTING IN THE NEW FRONTIER

++++++++++++++

Today finds me in a coffee shop with a table full of books and articles about the transformative potential of small-scale entrepreneurship, church planting in high-density cities, and the role of apostolic leaders in starting church planting networks. I've been devouring content as I work on writing a church planting strategy for North America that encapsulates everything I've written about in this book thus far.

As one who is wired for obscurity and desires to see church planting efforts in these off-the-beaten-path kinds of places, I am cognizant of the fact that much of the work ahead of me for creating strategies is on the theoretical end. Therefore, I am asking the question, "What does it mean to plant churches in these *new frontier* areas and communities?" My hope is that my strategy provides the answers. Recruitment, assessment, training, coaching, and mentoring are all geared towards that end. But first, what would, could, or should it look like to plant churches in this moving target of the new frontier?

Oakridge, Oregon

Meet Oakridge, Oregon. Population: 3,200.

Why Oakridge? What about urban neighborhoods and districts? Again, as a strategy we're looking at areas and people that are currently under-reached, marginalized, or under-emphasized. Oakridge certainly qualifies. Also, I view the community as I would an urban neighborhood. My current neighborhood in Portland has under 2,000 people. Smaller towns are almost like geographically separated urban neighborhoods.

Oakridge is located about forty miles southeast of Eugene. Its storyline is similar to many boom-and-bust communities whose economies were dependent upon mining, oil, fishing, or in this case, logging. The latter half of the twentieth century saw the mills close down and the community spiral downward economically.

Since everything is connected, what happens to a community economically impacts its citizens socially. When more and more workers are laid off, what happens? Domestic violence goes up. Drug and alcohol abuse rates skyrocket. Poverty amasses more people and the downward cycle spirals faster. This is what happened in inner-city communities such as Detroit or South Chicago. Most of those impacted were blue-collar workers in the auto industry, steel mills, and so on. As those sites began closing and relocating to the suburbs or overseas, thousands upon thousands of workers were left unemployed. They had a skillset, but nowhere to use it.

So often when we see gang violence, drugs, prostitution, higher rates of domestic violence, and poverty in these communities, it is easy to be smug and point fingers. But what do you do when your whole livelihood has been torn from you? What do you do when your whole neighborhood crumbles because the leading employers have shut their doors? It is more complex and nuanced than we realize. Those who can, get out, while those who can't are stuck.

Although Oakridge, Oregon, is a small rural town, there are similarities between it and inner-city America before gentrification moved in. When its economic well dried up, it sent shock waves throughout the community. Problems arose. However, there were people within the community who envisioned a different future. Rather than resigning Oakridge to a future of decline and desperation, they began thinking about how the town could reinvent itself to capture tourism dollars and ultimately more investment. This is where mountain biking comes in.

Much has been written on Oakridge and this transformation. From mountain bike magazines such as *Bike* to online articles to university-led research projects, more and more people have noticed what is happening in this rural Oregon community as well as in other similar communities across North America. In the context of this book, this is where we intersect with not only church planting, but also with the implications of a

"Father Kino" approach to church planting in terms of doing *more* than simply launching worship services. You see, there is an economic and social component to all of this as well.

The Mission of the Church

Ultimately this conversation is about our understanding of not only the mission of the church but the nature of the gospel. Christopher Wright asks these poignant questions: "Do the people of God have any responsibility to the rest of human society in general beyond evangelism? What content do we put into biblical phrases like 'being a blessing to the nations,' or 'seeking the welfare of the city,' or 'being the salt of the earth' or 'the light of the world,' or 'doing good' (one of the common expressions used by Paul and Peter)?"[1] The way we answer those questions determines *everything* about our approach to mission, the gospel, and yes, church planting.

I can make the case that what distinguishes Father Kino's story and his approach from that of the modern-day church planter is how one views the nature of God's mission. How we answer the questions "What is the gospel?" and "What is God's mission?" will reveal much about not just how we go about our daily lives, but how we conceive of and engage in church planting, gospel proclamation, and gospel demonstration. Looking at the story and example below will reveal one

---

[1] Wright, *The Mission of God's People*, 28.

way to rethink and wrestle with the question, "What is God's mission?"

Mountain Bike Oregon

This past summer, I was excited to get down to Oakridge. For years, Mountain Bike Oregon has operated as a mountain-biking festival that attracts riders from far and wide. Every day buses load up mountain bikers and their bikes and deposit them atop mountains from which they ride amazing Oregon singletrack back to town. This process is repeated daily for several days. In the evenings there are festivities and food. It's like Woodstock or Coachella for mountain bikers (including lots of hungover riders in the morning).

My reason for heading down was related to my coffee roasting company. Since everything we do is mountain bike-oriented, we connect with other companies, vendors, and riders all over the world. One of the companies we've connected with is an apparel company out of southern California. The plan was for me to brew and serve coffee in their booth.

It was a lot of fun to connect with other riders and serve them a free hot cup of coffee. More than one hungover rider appreciated the offer. They had to shake off the cobwebs because the shuttle buses would be leaving soon for another day of shredding trails and bombing hills.

By mid-morning, most of the riders had already departed and there was only one thing for us to do ... go for a ride ourselves. Since there were five us, we had multiple vehicles which allowed us to do a shuttled run down the popular Alpine trail. After driving an hour up, we arrived at the trailhead. Upon arriving we stretched, put on helmets and knee pads, and then dropped into the trail. It was fifteen miles and an hour and a half of whoops and hollers. We arrived back at the basecamp grinning from ear to ear. It was the cap to a perfect day.

I packed up my gear and set out for another highlight (at least for me)—to continue exploring Oakridge. I'm always curious to check out the latest happenings in the town. Any new developments? Businesses? Obviously, a quick drive around won't reveal much, but even the little we observe can be very revealing.

I still saw a small town struggling to reinvent itself. However, that's a sentiment not shared by everyone. Some would question why this community needs to cater to over-privileged mountain bikers? What is needed, they contend, is to find a way to rekindle the logging industry and reopen the mills. The result is some underlying tension.

Armed with my homegrown sociological powers of observation, I stepped into a fast food joint. I watched and listened to the young teens working behind the counter. I couldn't help but see in their eyes and faces what I saw when I looked in the mirror as a teenager—a longing to get out, to escape. I had that same look and mindset when I left my hometown for college vowing to never return other than for an occasional visit. I knew right away that Oakridge, just like many other places in small-town America, was still struggling and that for many young people, the goal is to get out. At least, to make it to Eugene 40 minutes away.

This story reveals the need of and the impetus behind a Father Kino approach to church planting. Not only are we interested in the spiritual lives of those who live there, but we're also interested and involved in placemaking and living out Jeremiah 29 in a community that has been in economic decline. However, since it's an uncool place it is left off the radar of most church planters in terms of a viable place for church planting and mission.

Church Planting in Uncool Places

This reveals the tension of church planting and engaging in mission in places like Oakridge. Most of us, whether we grew up rurally or not, still opt for and end up in cities. Economically-speaking, as I've shared previously, the chasm between cities and rural America keeps growing. This is true not only in terms of economics, but also in being able to access amenities such as healthcare, educational opportunities, and the like. Because of that, it is getting more and more difficult to find and recruit church planters to these locales, unless the communities have already flipped and become destination places such as Telluride, Park City, and Aspen, among others.

I've painfully detailed in *Urban Hinterlands: Planting the Gospel in Uncool Places* that my love for the glitz and glamor of cool cities has waned. That does not mean I don't enjoy and appreciate living in the heart of Portland. Nor does it mean that I don't enjoy our simple urban lifestyle, having access to endless urban amenities, and having the freedom to travel by foot, bike, or scooter. I enjoy and appreciate this city, and as soon as I start to find myself a bit jaded, I'm always reminded of how spectacular a place this truly is.

However, it doesn't always stir my heart in the way that struggling communities do. Again, an odd confession. For many, a move to Portland is a dream come true. I get that. But I'm wired for the long process of building and creating stuff, to see what's struggling turn around, and to see the forgotten become known. I pull constantly for the underdog.

It is no surprise then that places like Oakridge or Bisbee, Arizona, or my hometown of Tama, Iowa, fascinate, intrigue, and compel me. In terms of ministry and church planting, the floodgates are open for planters wanting to move to places like Portland. But who wants to go to Oakridge, Bisbee, or Tama? And even if they do go there, will they go in a spirit of resignation, as if these towns were like the last kids to be picked for a playground game of kickball? Or will they go with excitement, precisely because they were *not* cool, trendy, or alluring?

Really though. Its easy to nod my head, but what difference can I ACTUALLY make in these places. That I'm drawn to?

Geographic Ramifications of Mission

How to we bring encouragement & hope?

The geography of mission is not static. It is like a river that over the millennia changes its course, creates new bends and sandbars, and cuts new channels. Throughout the brief modern history of missions, we've seen this: from coastal communities to pushing inland, to the 10/40 window, to cities, and so on. Each successive wave is in some ways a continuation and a course correction from the previous wave. Now that we've gone all-in on cities, particularly larger ones, we've left in their wake tens of thousands of smaller communities. These places are no longer considered viable for church planting because rural America as a whole is in serious economic decline.

I can be very business minded - but "the good news"- what is it? Can life spark for the church? Can the church spark Creative, innovative Change to a town & community that trans- forms the whole attitude & outlook - eventually the town itself becomes, better.

Some communities are dying as their local economies decline. Young people simply up and leave. Alana Semuels notes in her article "The Graying of Rural America":

> Population decline in rural America is especially concentrated in the West. There's a lot of wide-open land there, but most people, and young people especially, live in the cities. Half the jobs in Oregon, for example, are now in three counties in

and around Portland, according to a study by Headwaters. Almost two-thirds of Utah's jobs are along the Wasatch Front, which runs from Salt Lake City to Provo.[2]

This is the reality of places like Oakridge and Bisbee. However, in the face of decline, what we're also finding is that these struggles and tensions can bring out the best in the human spirit:

> Now, locals are being urged to start their own businesses. Since 1970, the number of self-employed individuals grew 178 percent, according to Headwaters's analysis. And this is during a period of incredible decline. Locals have started businesses like small handmade-salsa companies and microbreweries, Greg Smith, the head of the Wheeler County Economic Development Corporation, said.
>
> "These folks are resilient," he said. "They're very self-sustaining, smart people, and they are going to make the decisions they need to make to continue living in frontier Oregon."[3]

How can the church be a part of this? What if we entered into these kinds of communities (whether urban or rural) with a whole new framework and set of tools and skills? That

---

[2] Semuels, "The Graying of Rural America," para. 11.
[3] Ibid., 38–39.

doesn't mean there won't be challenges and enormous obstacles. This narrative looks drastically different in different parts of the country and from state to state and community to community.

There are still thousands of strong towns and communities, but those that are struggling are using a new (to them) moniker to describe their bleak outlook. Recently I stumbled across an article on NPR titled "Doctor Shortage In Rural Arizona Sparks Another Crisis In 'Forgotten America.'" It even highlights one of the communities I've been writing about—Bisbee. Here's a key exchange in the article:

> "Copper from Bisbee, Ariz., is what helped win World War I," [Bisbee mayor] Smith says. "And yet, when we are in need, we are forgotten because it's not convenient — and because it's not a whole bunch of people here that are voters."

Over at Bisbee's Copper Queen Community Hospital, CEO James Dickson goes further.

He sees the doctor shortage as the latest example of why people in towns like this are feeling left behind, untouched by the economic booms in many American cities. It's a likely contributor to the country's growing economic and cultural divide, Dickson says.

> "They're starting to call the rural areas 'the new inner city' because we have the

same shortages and lack of access to care," he says.

How do you have a thriving economy if you don't have access to health care?[4]

One of the most poignant statements is this idea that "They're starting to call rural areas 'the new inner city.'" The first time I read that it jolted me. How do we recall the inner cities of a generation ago? The answer: higher concentrations of poverty, a lack of access to amenities and services, economic exclusion, substandard living conditions in terms of housing, and so on. More and more rural areas are moving in this direction.

I saw this on a visit last year to my hometown of Tama, Iowa. It was unsettling to see its physical decline. While it had never been glamorous, it now looked faded, distressed, shuttered, and trending downward. Our beloved downtown was filled mostly with closed businesses. It was sad.

Welcome to one of the new frontiers in church planting in North America. It's neither trendy, nor cool, nor overly alluring to the ambitious young church planter. But maybe that's why it's truly part of the new frontier in church planting, since it'll take intrepid souls willing to roll up their sleeves and jump in.

---

[4] Siegler, "Doctor Shortage In Rural Arizona Sparks Another Crisis in 'Forgotten America,'" para. 15-19.

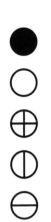

6

__ __ __ __ __ __ __

WHERE DID WE
VEER OFF COURSE?

+++++++++++++

Where did we veer off course? This is the dilemma in North American missions. When we look back to men like Father Kino, we see an early missionary ethos. Now in fairness they *were* operating as "conventional" missionaries. Meaning, they were foreign-born and came *here* to spread the gospel and plant churches. One then may argue, as in Kino's case, that he was operating under the umbrella of Christendom. He had to leave his home in Italy in order to be a cross-cultural missionary in "godless" North America. But how are we to view North America today? Particularly, in places that outsiders still view as "godless."

One of the common myths that outsiders have about the Pacific Northwest is that there was never a gospel presence in cities like Portland, Seattle, and Vancouver, British Columbia. While that sounds great when marketing the region to potential church planters and support churches, it is simply not true. There have been notable revivals in these cities. In fact, during the first part of the twentieth century, one revival in Portland was so extensive that the shipping docks were shut down during the lunch hour because the workers were studying the Bible and being radically saved.

Another myth is that not only were we a unified American nation, but that from the beginning we were a Christian nation. Current pleas to "get back to our roots" when America was "one nation under God" are misinformed. Colin Woodard writes in *American Nations*:

> When society was turned upside down by mass immigration at the turn of both the twentieth and twenty-first centuries, intellectuals counseled that America was in danger of losing the 'Anglo-Protestant' culture and associated 'American creed' that had supposedly kept the nation unified.[1]

But have we ever been a unified and culturally cohesive nation? Woodard goes on:

> Such calls for unity overlook a glaring historical fact: Americans have been deeply divided since the days of Jamestown and Plymouth. The original North American colonies were settled by people from distinct regions of the British Islands, and from France, the Netherlands, and Spain, each with their own religious, political, and ethnographic characteristics. Throughout the colonial period, they regarded one another as competitors--and occasionally as enemies ... All of these centuries-old cultures are still with us today, and have spread their people, ideas,

---

[1] Woodard, *American Nations*, 1.

and influence across mutually exclusive bands of the continent. *There isn't and never has been one America, but rather several Americas.*[2]

You see, we've always been a nation of immigrants. The only difference now is that the countries of origin have changed. Whereas most immigrants were once of European descent, many today are coming from non-white nations—from Mexico or Iran, Sudan or Thailand.

I believe that part of the undercurrent of the awakening realization that North America truly is a mission field is that many new immigrants are not from European Christendom. In addition, their cultures and mannerisms seem alien to many. This movement of peoples is re-orienteering how we live in and experience our cities. I am not saying by any stretch that this is a new phenomenon. Portland's historic Chinatown is a reminder that from early on this has been a city of immigrants, whether from the east coast, Europe, or Asia. But current immigration has triggered a growing desire among many in church planting and missions to minister to this global diaspora that's now residing in our cities. They continue to open our eyes to the fact that we truly *are* living on the mission field.

This notion is neither noteworthy nor new, but for many Americans this wake-up call is nonetheless unsettling. They have grown up in

---

[2] Ibid., 2. Italics mine.

churches with a passion for international missions—to go overseas to serve God and be a missionary. However, all along there has been this unspoken truth that where we live is the mission field and always has been. Obviously, this conversation will be different depending on where one lives in the US. Some places will feel the brunt of this conversation more acutely than others. Living in the heart of Portland I don't have the luxury of thinking and acting as if I'm in some modern-day Christendom. That doesn't mean that God is not at work. It is simply different.

Up to now in this book, I've attempted to explore and document the changing frontier of missions in North America. For many cities, I'd contend that the frontier is still the city center, while for others it's in the "new" suburbs. What I mean by "new" is this: In Portland, for example, the heart of the city is predominantly white and middle class (and hipster). However, travel east of 82nd Street or out to Gresham, and all of a sudden there are growing numbers of international immigrants, refugees, and minorities.

Exploring the Dichotomy

So where did we veer off course? As soon as we began thinking that the *mission field* was all over *there* and *ministry* was all right *here*. That is not to be dismissive of the great missionary movement of the previous century in which tens of thousands of missionaries went out from North

America. But when the narrative became all about *going* to do missions instead of *staying* to do missions, that's when this unhealthy dichotomy became entrenched. I will always contend that it isn't either/or but both/and. We are *always* on mission no matter where in the world we live.

This chapter is not a diatribe or rant against the church. I love the church. God has used the North American church mightily and she is still his bride. However, that does not mean we don't need a course correction from time to time or even on a regular basis. I always point out that the reason why we have Paul's letters to the churches in the New Testament is because these churches had veered off course and needed a course correction. His motive was love and his desire was to bring them back to health and mission. We need that today.

It is easy for us to become entrenched, especially when that entrenchment is slightly off from where we need to be. I look back now on my last twenty-plus years of following Christ. It seems like I've experienced one course correction after another. I begin heading down a path—a different way of thinking, a mindset, a habit, or something destructive—and then along the way I become convicted, challenged, or confronted by the realization that I have veered off course. Once that happens, I have only two options. Ignore the evidence before me and continue on my way, or stop, heed the Spirit's wisdom, and repent.

Sometimes these course corrections are simply breaking through old habits that are not necessarily wrong but are simply out of date. I vividly recall in my early twenties a moment when I was confronted with my own resistance to change. No one had confronted me. But the world around me was changing and I was not comfortable. From music tastes to fashion to culture I was losing step with the world around me. An odd admission for someone in his early twenties at the time.

This angst surfaced one day as I was watching an NBA game. I grew up with the likes of Magic, Jordan, and Bird. Basketball was "supposed" to look, feel, and be played a "certain" way. By my twenties I began noticing a change in the culture of the NBA. The game opened up, players began getting tattoos (shocker!) all over, and what I knew of the NBA from my childhood was disappearing. I resisted. I didn't like it. I was frustrated. I felt like an entrenched, grumpy old man. I actually was. I had stopped changing.

Then I had my "breakthrough." All of a sudden it dawned on me that the world is constantly changing before my eyes, and that unless I change with it, I will be left behind. I was scared. You see, we all know people who have stopped changing, whether it was when they were in their twenties, thirties, forties, or whenever. They stopped listening to new music, they longed for the "good old days," and become more and more resistant to the changes going on around them. I almost

went that route in my twenties. There's a
difference between aging and getting old.

It was a 180-degree course correction for me. I
had previously been inflexible, but I learned to be
culturally pliable. My entrenchment was not a
concerted effort or even noticeable. It "just
happened." No bad intentions. No purposeful
dismissal of the new. Just a sense of being
comfortable with what I knew and having no
desire to "keep up."

I would contend that the same applies to the
church. The world around us is changing at a
break-neck speed and oftentimes we don't like it.
It's as if when we finally figure something out, we
think we're OK. The seeker-sensitive church was
big in the 80s and 90s, but today it looks a bit
foolish. Why? Because the culture has changed.

Each course correction for the church is
fraught with struggle, conflict, and angst. Usually
the tension is that some churches go too far while
some don't go far enough. The debates heat up as
a proliferation of books and articles appear
seeking to address the raging issue. Seemingly as
soon as the ink on the pages dries, the culture has
shifted again. And yet after a decade, we're still
haggling over something that is no longer
relevant. It is at this point (and at many other
points along the way) that we have to decide: will
we keep changing or will we stay put?

Contextualization

Missiologically-speaking, this is what we mean by contextualizing. However, many assume that it is a one-time deal. Much effort can go into the contextualization process when launching out on a church-planting endeavor. Once the church is birthed, it's assumed that there is no longer a need for contextualization. Hopefully you're beginning to see how untrue that is. In reality, a church should be in a constant state of hammering through the process of contextualization.

What happens when a church doesn't keep contextualizing? The affects are all around us, in each and every city and town: churches that are antiquated, entrenched, and resistant to change. We call them "traditional" churches or "legacy" churches. That sounds nice, but the reality is that they stopped changing and, more importantly, they stopped contextualizing. Recent history shows that every new church expression will someday soon become old and out of date—the seeker church, the emerging church, and so many other labels that I've lost track.

I don't think there was simply one time or place in the history of the American church where we veered off course. The *whole* American church is not off-base missiologically. Sure, there are plenty that are. But the challenge is that every church is in danger of veering off course unless they continuously wrestle with the culture and how to contextualize it. Even ten years after a new church expression is birthed, if it does not reinvent itself and readdress its posture relative to the ever-changing culture, then it's at risk of becoming entrenched and obsolete.

We're all creatures of habit. Even something silly like the kind of facial hair a man sports is reflective of an era. When I see fifty-year-olds donning a soul patch, it takes me back to the late 1990s and early 2000s. Sure, everything is cyclical and what goes around comes around, but the point is that it is easy for us to get stuck in a past era or way of thinking. That is why a full-blown seeker church is typically full of primarily Baby Boomers.

The point is that we're not called to be a seeker church, an organic church, a house church, an emerging church, a pulpit-centered church, or anything like that. Instead we're called to be contextual. Who's the biggest hang-up in this conversation for pastors and church planters? We are. US. *We're* the hang-up! You see, most of us subscribe to and love a certain way of doing and being the church. It makes sense to us, we like it, we're fans of it, and we'll roll with it. I know way too many church planters who are enamored with preaching and spend fifteen hours a week in sermon prep as if that mode of teaching and communication comes from Scripture. They are so culture-bound to a tradition that they cannot fathom thinking any other way.

Conversely, there are many who are so enraptured with the [*Insert current movement here*] way of doing and being the church that they cannot imagine it any other way. Either way, we have such a love for models that we are simply not willing to do the hard work of contextualization beyond paying it lip service. Contextualization is painful. Now you can see why it is so easy to veer off course in terms of mission.

Church history reveals how entrenched this struggle really is. Every tradition and expression of church was probably at one time contextual and resonated with the culture. But as the story of my early 20s shows, it is easy to get stuck and stop adapting. Most of us can point back to a time in church history where to our minds they "nailed it" – whether it be houses churches in the first century, the liturgical post-Constantine Roman Catholic Church, the Reformation, the Wesleyan movement, American Pentecostalism, and so on–– and then attempt to do church accordingly. We plant our flags and assume we don't need to keep contextualizing. But as I said, *every* expression of church we see now will in some way and at some point become antiquated and out of touch with the cultural reality. We scoff at older generations for their attachment to tradition and the dying churches that resulted. But if we don't adapt, that will be our fate too in twenty, forty, or sixty years.

So where did the North American church veer off course? There was no single spot, but compromises and resistance occur on a daily basis. Course corrections need to be ongoing and regular.

7

_ _ _ _ _ _ _

WHAT ARE WE
DOING?

+++++++++++++

I love church planters. Seriously, I do. I have given the last fifteen years of my life to church planting in various roles and capacities. I am now at the point where everything I see and analyze is through the lens of church planting.

Most of the people I will meet up with over coffee in a given week are church planters. It consumes my writing as well as thoughts, strategies, and longings. I am committed to it. As a result, I feel that I can sincerely shine a light on aspects of how we train and deploy church planters. Not out of personal angst or a desire to berate and be contentious, but because I love my fellow church planters and I long for us all to be more effective wherever God would lead us.

This chapter comprises my own State of the Union address regarding the current state of church planting. The fact that I'm in North America will necessarily narrow my focus. I want to assess the current situation by trying to answer several basic questions: *Why* do our church planting methods differ depending on whether the setting is domestic (here) or foreign (there)? *Why* do we think of church planting differently *here as opposed to there*? *Why* do we view church planters differently *here as opposed to there?*

Why do we assume different habits or roles for church planters *here as opposed to there?*

The categories that I will explore within the context of this dichotomy are: training, calling, identity, methods, and lifestyle.

Training

Right out of the gate, I contend that we still don't do a very good job of training church planters. As I will get into in the next chapter, while there is a wide variety of training materials and methodologies out there, we're either too model-driven or we simply deal with abstracts versus on-the-ground topics such as how to map or exegete cities and cultivate our walk with God. Lately I've been re-reading a book by Roger Barrier that I first read fifteen years ago. He states, "The seminary I attended required approximately thirty classes for a Master of Divinity degree. As I recall, not a single class explained how to hear God speak. Looking back, I see that my seminary experience was focused on becoming biblically smart and ministerially efficient. Cultivating the spiritual life was an afterthought."[1] That quote summarizes well the many conversations I've had with recent seminary grads.

The point is that there are all kinds of gaps in our training. I see it all the time when I meet with church planters. Some come in with robust

---

[1] Barrier, *Listening to the Voice of God*, 23.

theological training. Others have no formal biblical or theological training and are simply figuring out church planting on the fly. Others have been through training that pushes them towards a non-contextualized model that was developed in another city in another part of the country.

As I survey church planters, I would say that *most* have not even been trained. They have simply been sent out. Since church planters are pretty savvy, they end up picking up pieces along the way; but rarely do I find a planter who has had any kind of significant church planting training. And even less often do I find one who possesses the tools to help them along the way, such as cultural exegesis, contextualization, mapping, evangelism, and more. They usually latch on to a book or two, although most would rather read books on preaching and church growth.

The point is that if there is any kind of training, it is usually something along the lines of preaching or planning attractive worship gatherings and church growth. I rarely find much training on a missionary posture that encourages, challenges, and equips planters to effectively study their context and to plant contextual churches. Instead, we and they end up leading first with models and then offering the "how-tos" related to those models.

Calling

It seems that in every book I write, this topic of calling comes up again and again. Why is that? Here's a little clue: Whenever someone focuses *a lot* on a certain topic, it usually means they are either wrestling or struggling with it, or fascinated and overjoyed by it, or both. You hear it in sermons and you find it in books. I am guilty as charged since I'm both fascinated and haunted by God's calling.

For me, calling has a geographic component to it. While many planters are called to a region or a city, we (and I include myself) need to wrestle with things beyond "I feel called to plant a church in Portland." There needs to be a good sifting and sorting. Healthy and robust. Not a second-guessing and always questioning. Since this comes up regularly during my week, let me share a couple of examples.

Interestingly, since moving to Portland I've had a few conversations with people discerning a call to move back to Tucson to plant a church. Early in the process we somehow got connected. Last week I had coffee with a local pastor who is feeling the tug of God to move to Tucson. Within this discernment process, the issue is not only whether to pastor an existing church or plant a new one, but also *where*. It's fine to have a generalized calling to Tucson, but the next questions are: *where* and *among whom*?

I came away feeling greatly encouraged that the places under consideration were not cool, nor sexy, nor well-churched. Too often I find planters, once they've identified a city where they feel God calling them, simply selecting neighborhoods that they "like."

I put "like" in quotation marks because most church planters say they're drawn to the same parts of the city and the same neighborhoods. Within a three-day span I had multiple conversations with either brand new church planters or ones moving to Portland within the next year. All of them were either making plans or had already begun to plant in the *same* neighborhood. And in this neighborhood, there are already other new churches, as well as the campuses of several larger churches. I'd contend that while they had a generalized calling to Portland, they still needed to burrow deeper into *where* in Portland. Why? Because while the cool and desirable parts of the city receive *most* of the new church planters, the uncool and undesirable neighborhoods continue to be forgotten.

Identity

This is where the divergence really begins. What is the identity of a church planter? Who or what is a church planter? The answers to these questions can reveal a lot. They also help determine a church planter's habits and lifestyle. The answers, in other words, are foundational.

I've grown to differentiate between a church planter and a missionary. The question for each and every church planter is: do you see yourself in essence as a pastor planting a church or as a missionary? What happens when they answer this question? What changes? In a word, *everything*.

Imagine you're sitting around a table with a group of ministry leaders whom you've never met before. One by one they introduce themselves and share what they do. Then the leaders ask questions because they're eager to learn more about one another. When your turn comes, you answer, "My name is _____ and I am *planting a church* in _____." Let's now imagine what the focus would be when people begin asking more questions. We know in general where this conversation is going, right?

Usually the questions that leaders ask are:

- What part of the city are you planting in?
- How is your core group developing?
- Have you launched yet?
- When do you plan on launching?
- What will your services be like?
- Have you done any preview services?
- Are you utilizing public interest meetings?
- What are you doing for marketing? Direct mailers? Social media?
- Will you preach exegetically or topically?

While these questions may or may not chafe the church planter, they are all fair game. Sure, there are a few other questions interspersed that I did not list here, but you get the idea. Self-identifying as a "church planter" assumes a lot about what that means.

Now let's alter that same scenario. You're still a "church planter" (whatever that now means), but you answer like this: "My name is _____ and I am a *missionary* in _____." Now the entire narrative changes. Rather than the others at the table peppering you with questions about worship services, core groups, and preaching, the questions become more like:

- What does it mean to be a missionary in your city?
- How are you engaging with people in your neighborhood?
- Have you become an insider yet?
- What platform are you utilizing to make deeper connections in your city and to establish a presence?
- What does it look like to share the gospel there? How open or resistant are people to Jesus?
- What aspect of culture in your city can you tap into in order to bring up spiritual conversations and ultimately point people to Jesus?

Obviously, I'm using those specific questions to make a point. While they're not exclusive to either side, what this little scenario demonstrates is that *how* church planters self-identify will reveal much about their approach to church planting. Too often church planters want to simply hurry up the launch of their public worship services so that they can do what they really want to do, which is focus on sermon prep, plan the services, and preach.

Nate Morches, in an article entitled "The Apostle Paul was Not a Pastor, and You Might Not Really Be One Either" explores this dichotomy. He differentiates between how we think of pastors (which he denotes as "elders") versus apostolic church planters (the Pauline leaders). He writes, "But the main difference between elders and Pauline leaders was this: Elders stayed in one location to manage their single church, while Pauline leaders moved between the churches to act as a strengthening force and a connection between all the churches."[2] This identity difference is at the crux of identifying someone as either a church-planting pastor (or elder) or a church-planting missionary (or apostle).

Methods

I am hesitant to share this next thought because I don't want my words to be

---

[2] Morsches, "The Apostle Paul Was Not a Pastor, and You Might Not Really Be One Either," para. 16.

misconstrued as arrogant or anything like that. Far from it. A number of years ago, I stopped reading books on church planting, going to church-planting conferences, and reading blogs or articles on the subject. Why? Because I've arrived and I think I know it all? Hardly. Besides, I wasn't that good as a planter myself, so I have no room to boast. What did turn me off was the proliferation of *group-think*.

Group-think basically means that everyone ends up parroting the few with a common narrative of what church planting is or should be. The way this plays out is that when there are successful examples, the methodology gets repeated over and over again. It becomes entrenched. Context becomes irrelevant. As a result, the group-thinkers have crafted a "good understanding" of the methodology church planters use or at least *should use.*

In the process, innovation gets left behind and everyone becomes a copycat. At best, innovation is reduced to a tweak or an adaptation of some tried-and-true method or technique. The result is that blogs, articles, books, and conferences all begin looking and sounding the same regardless of the spin put on them.

This observation is at the crux of my appeal for missionary thinking. Missionaries need to be pliable. If we as church planters go in with a predetermined plan void of context, we end up jettisoning it after we land at our destination.

Today I find too many planters simply parroting and not innovating. Besides, who would dare contradict the church-planting sages of our day? To do so would be foolish ... right?

I see on websites and across social media that we continue to engage in church planting in the same way we've always done it. Obviously in some contexts this is good missiology, while in others it is not. This is not to be dismissive of historical Christianity, nor to disregard Scriptural imperatives for the church; but we also have to admit that we're already coloring outside of the lines, since most of our methods are not found in the New Testament. Meaning, we've adapted and contextualized. However, we need to give ourselves permission (under the authority of Scripture) to continue to contextualize our methods.

Lifestyle

The question before church planters is: how are they (we) to live? What should a typical day or week look like for a church planter? Obviously, the answers to these questions will be influenced mostly by context, but there are some commonalities across the board. You see, everything to this point becomes cumulative. Once the whole trajectory gets set in motion, then all the dominos begin falling.

I would contend that the lifestyle of church planters is a direct reflection of their training, calling, identity, and of course methods. Maybe a church planter is not sure initially of their identity and how they see themselves, but there's a good chance that their training, funding, and all the other strings attached will push them in a certain direction. Maybe a better way to differentiate these two modes of church planting, which depend on calling and identity, would be to call one a church-planter pastor and the other a church-planter missionary.

Just because one identifies as the former doesn't mean they're done planting once their church is established. Nor does being the latter mean that they are always on the move and rarely stay put in one place for more than a couple of years. However, there is a direct correlation between the identities of both and their vastly different lifestyles.

When I meet with church-planting pastors, the conversations revolve entirely around the *church*. We talk about the worship gatherings, leadership development, ornery parishioners, people leaving the church, problems with the worship team, finding affordable spaces for the worship gatherings, multiplying small groups, following a certain liturgical calendar, sermon preparation, dealing with church finances, and more. That focus, in turn, dictates and influences the planters' lifestyle.

Conversely, a church-planting missionary lives a different lifestyle. How so? One way to see would be to answer the following questions. What is the lifestyle of a pastor? What is the lifestyle of a missionary? The answers to those questions will often be significantly different. Many missionaries I know and meet simply *do* different things. They go to places like Nepal and begin an urban gardening co-op as a way to connect with people. They move to Thailand to start a bike shop to create a community hub as a way to connect with people. They move to Mexico and start a kayak guiding service to connect with people. They move to Turkey to launch a specialty coffee shop to connect with people.

While both work towards the same goal (establishing new churches), their lifestyles, methods, and habits differ noticeably. I also believe that what distinguishes the two is how they view their career or occupation. For most planters, it's about establishing a new church in hopes of it paying a salary as soon as possible. Thus, one of the unspoken goals is to establish and grow the church quickly and in such a way that it begins meeting their financial needs. For many, church planting is a career move.

So where does this leave us in our conversation about the state of church planting? My purpose here has simply been to bring to light many of the unspoken assumptions about church planting. This is not to cast guilt or shame or anything like that. It is simply an assessment. In the next chapter, while I may seek to push us in the direction of being church-planting missionaries, the fact remains that *most* of the current training systems and material push people in the direction of being church-planting pastors.

8

_ _ _ _ _ _ _

WHERE ARE WE GOING?

++++++++++++++

What does it mean to train church planters and ultimately how do we quantify the effectiveness of their training? As I set out to explore these questions, I do so with humility and grace. I'm not asking these questions from a distance, but as someone who regularly teaches and trains church planters. In other words, in tackling this subject, I am also examining my own leanings and biases, and the outcomes of my own teaching.

I could cite example after example of people I know—pastors, church planters, and other ministry leaders—who finished seminary only to realize that their training did not suffice. In fact, apart from classes in languages, theology, and the Bible, they didn't really gain much practical experience that prepared them for a life of ministry. I highly value seminary training and higher education. After all, I am a professor. I also readily admit that my life was transformed by my education as it taught me to think, wrestle intellectually, and develop the theological foundation that I am still building on to this day. In other words, this chapter is not intended to bash nor berate nor belittle anyone or anything. I am part of the academic community, not someone firing shots at the ship.

We are all wired differently. That means we learn differently. It is more than being an auditory learner versus a visual learner versus a kinesthetic learner. We learn and grasp things so differently from one other that no one can claim that there is a one-size-fits-all training method. I'm a reader. I don't do well at sitting and listening. Sunday church gatherings are hard for me. I have to fight with everything I have to stay engaged. I'd much rather mess around on social media or check out the sports scores or watch games on my phone. Does that make me shallow? Maybe. Maybe not. But I learn best by reading voraciously. The only time I listen to teachings or sermons is on a podcast while I'm riding my bike, roasting coffee, or washing dishes. I need to be active while listening. If not, I'll fidget and become bored.

If I'm like this, how can I dare to assume that there's only one way to train planters? I remember sitting atop a hotel in Xi'an, China, listening to an underground house church "uncle" talking about church planting movements and the explosive growth of the church in China. One of those in my group of doctoral students asked him, "How do you train church planters?" The church leader looked baffled by the question. He replied, "We don't train people to plant churches. When people become Christians, we teach them the Bible and immediately send them out in pairs to other villages to preach the gospel." Church planting for them was simply a byproduct of evangelism. No training, no strategy apart from discipleship. In fact, church planting was for them simply *part* of their discipleship process and what it means to follow Jesus.

Now, could we in North America do that today? Would that work in educated urban contexts? Maybe. Maybe not. But the point is that there are many ways to train church planters.

Church Planting Training Systems Collected

In preparation for writing this book, I collected training materials from over twelve different denominations, church-planting networks and organizations (and that number continues to grow). This represents a great cross-section of training approaches, and most of them are well-known throughout the US and Canada as well as globally. I will *not* reveal who they are from. The reason? I want to honor their work in training and mobilizing church planters. These are great organizations doing great work in the Kingdom. That allows me to *critique* them (which is different from criticizing them) in a way that still upholds their work. Also, many have entrusted me with their confidential materials. I want to honor that.

As I've noted throughout this book, I admittedly come to this conversation with my own bias, grid, or framework. Meaning, I'm using the example of Father Kino as my interpretive lens. As a researcher, I know this can skew the results. However, we all have our biases and we all come to the table with our own leanings, preferences, culture, and so on. I want to be upfront with mine.

As I read through the materials, what was immediately noticeable was how church planters were trained—and how they were *not* trained. The similarity, despite minor variances in theological frameworks, was that the bulk of the training centered around the gospel, missional theology, building community, and spiritual formation. In other words, most church planters were trained in the "soft skills" of theology, Bible, and discipleship. For Christians like those in Xi'an, China, that would seem to be sufficient. But I wonder if that would suffice for other church planters in other contexts?

The materials I studied yielded these key headings:

- The Gospel Story
- Missional theology
- Missional ecclesiology
- Community formation (missional communities)
- Leadership
- Marketing
- Launching public worship services

Obviously, each of those broad categories are essential. I'm sure no one would disagree, me included. So what's the problem? The problem is not with what is there, but with what is *not* there. Nitpicking? Sure.

On the other hand, in those instances where the training did get practical and specific, it tended to be presented as a how-to manual for planting conventional attractional churches. The focus was on developing a core group, the lead up to the public launch, how to move to two services, preaching, planning out worship song sets, marketing, and the like. Since I'm a firm believer that it takes all kinds of churches to reach all kinds of people, I'm not advocating "simple" churches versus "attractional" church or anything like that.

One of the high-water marks of the attractional church would have to be Saddleback Church in Orange County, California. While many today make a sport out of poking holes in such churches, my experiences have always been to the contrary. The first time I ever visited Saddleback in the late-90s I sat in the back and wept. It was a powerful and moving experience. I had a strong sense of God's love and presence. I stayed in my seat through the next service.

I am an advocate for almost all kinds of churches in all shapes and sizes. My critique is more on the subterranean level. More than simply making up a generic list of what a church should or should not have and do, and ticking all the boxes you can, I would contend that how we train church planters reflects how we view the world— in particular, cities and our role within them. It is easy to talk about the church, church planting, core groups, public launch, song lists, social media and marketing, while never actually getting around to talking about the city, let alone a particular neighborhood.

What About Context?

I have sat through too many conversations with planters and trainers in which it seemed that context was merely an afterthought. Almost all of their energy and focus seemed to be on building up the church. While some organizations do mention and even train for evangelism, many seem preoccupied with building a church service. Rarely is context mentioned. It is as though where the church is located is secondary. The vision then becomes all about planting a great (read: *big*) church and how to do that, rather than seeking to uncover what ails the community, God's heart and vision for that community, and how this new church can make a positive difference. Yes, nitpicking for sure.

To be fair, some of these training materials do at least address context; but again, my interpretive lens is Father Kino. I can already imagine the pushback—*different context, wouldn't work today, he worked among traditional tribal societies, he came in from a position of power, and so on.* I get that. I am not blind to the mixed legacy of these Jesuit missionaries in the Americas. Some were wonderful and godly men, while others wielded ungodly power in abusive and corrupt ways.

I wonder what it would have been like for Kino if he had only been trained as we train church planters. While he would have been adept at celebrating the Mass, I don't believe his legacy would have been longstanding. But as a church-planting missionary, his legacy lives on across millennia and generations. For us, it all hinges on this question: Do we want to build a great *church* or a great *society*? Our answer to that question becomes pivotal in determining the path we choose. In my estimation, *most* of today's church-planting training focuses on how to build *great churches*. The naïve assumption is that a great church will in turn build or mold or shape a great society. Not so.

Yesterday morning I met up with a Master's grad in urban planning. He has a unique background because not only did he study regional urban planning, but he has also been involved in church planting. He's been in Portland for a year now and has plugged into a new well-known local church. As we were talking about some of the topics addressed in this book, he paused and said, "You know, it has finally dawned on me that according to my church, our role in the city is about evangelism. Apart from hearing about that on Sundays and once in a while serving food in one of the homeless shelters, no one is really talking about how to engage the city."

The poignancy of his statement is that his church is dedicated to being in and for the city, and yet the sole outcome of this dedication is evangelism. Can we at least conceive of the notion that God has his church in the city *not only* to evangelize, but also to seek its betterment, and that this absolutely entails serving and loving the homeless? There is *so much more* that we can and must do. But I'm afraid that our presuppositions and theological foundations for how we train our planters lead us to be more disengaged from the city than we'd like to admit.

Most of the training I've studied testifies to this.

Got Skills?

A typical potential church planter who goes through the typical training would have the skills to think theologically, gather and form missional (or gospel) communities, launch a public worship service for the spiritually-convinced, preach, lead, and write blogs and books about it all. It is a repeating cycle. No wonder few really break away from this now-common church-planting narrative. To do so would seem to most people scandalous, foolish, and naïve. And so we're stuck in a rut and our training does nothing to get us out of it.

I keep feeling the need to reiterate that I affirm our training. It's not that it is bad, simply underdeveloped. It would be like a student going through medical school learning all the textbook information about the human body, treatments, and the like, but *never* getting out on rotations or doing a residency. Sure, our seminaries offer students some degree of field experience, but most often it is limited to opportunities for preaching or leading a small group.

As I have mentioned repeatedly, if we send our missionaries overseas trained only to preach and lead small groups, we've done them *and* the people we're sending them to a great disservice. Instead, what if we trained missionaries (and planters) to also be entrepreneurs, to launch NGOs, dig wells, build high-end furniture, true wheels on a bike, and so much more?

Yes, this might seem like crazy thinking, but as we have already seen, things must change.

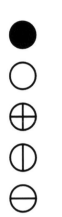

9

— — — — — — —

WHAT IS MISSING?

++++++++++++++

Recently I had coffee with a young ministry leader who had recently graduated from seminary. His education track went from doing an undergrad in biblical studies to a Masters of Divinity in pastoral ministries. That was the exact route that I had taken. He spent an hour talking about his work with troubled urban youth and all that that entails. But all the while, I kept turning the conversation back to his educational experience. I hope he didn't notice.

Sure enough, apart from Bible and theology classes, most of his "ministry" courses dealt with preaching and public speaking, counseling, and thinking/talking about culture. Again, these are all foundational and very important. But did that prepare him adequately for a life of ministry? Sure, having a solid foundation is pivotal since everything about who we are and what we do is built on that base. And yet I couldn't help but ask myself how much this young man had missed ... and to be honest, how much *I* had missed.

Knowing what I'd missed was part of my motivation to begin a PhD studying urban planning. I wanted *something* that was practical and relevant that went beyond theology and theory. Maybe someday I will pick that up again, but for now I have my hands full with my own creative start-ups. It's one more piece to add to the large crockpot of my mind like big chunks of meat, carrots, and potatoes that continue to simmer and cook. On the one hand, we need meaty chunks of the Bible and theology as part of our training. We also need the carrots of preaching, leading, counseling, discipling, and so on. But what about the potatoes? Where is the exposure of students to the *practical* skills that go beyond church planting?

This would be like the apostle Paul training church-planting missionaries how to make a decent tent. How often do we read in his letters about how Paul did not ask for offerings from his churches so that no one would question his motives? How often have we read that because he didn't want to be a financial burden to his churches, he also worked as a tentmaker even though he had every right to expect them to support him? But many church planters today seem to have that all backwards—working outside the church *is* the burden. Why? Because for most of them, including myself and the young man I mentioned earlier, it entails working some junk job they hate and dream of getting away from as soon as their church is big enough to pay them a full-time salary.

When Bivocationalism Works

For a while, when Starbucks used to be cool, many church planters I knew worked there for several years as baristas, shift supervisors, or managers while their new churches slowly grew. Over time, they would cut their hours from full-time to part-time and eventually quit when they were able to make the leap into the church full-time. Like Paul, they didn't want to be a burden to anyone, so they worked hard for the benefit of their churches *and* their families. Why did so many church planters opt to work at Starbucks? Because you didn't really need previous experience or education, and it provided insurance benefits.

While for many planters, it probably wasn't the career track that many had envisioned prior to getting into ministry, it ended up being valuable work experience. Even so, for most it was more like a purgatory than a joy. In other words, we rarely think as Paul did, being willing to do extra work even if he didn't have to. We just want a full-time gig prepping sermons, meeting one-on-one with people, planning events, and the like. I get that.

When I first ventured into church planting, I was in the same boat. My go-to line is that when I was a church planter, I was such a good fundraiser that I had to get a job. Before moving to Tucson, Arizona, to jump into church planting, I had been a youth pastor for five years. My undergrad degree was in biblical studies and I was working on a Master's in church planting and church growth. After locking into a two-year lease of a home and adding up the funds we had raised, I realized we needed more money. The funding wasn't enough to provide for my family.

This was a blow to my ego and identity. I had thrown my life into serving God full-time from the moment I surrendered my life to him as a teenager. I was all-in for serving him for the rest of my life. There was no turning back; it was ministry or bust. Now I was out from under the security of being on staff at a church. I was venturing out alone to plant a church from scratch.

So I got a job, as I mentioned in chapter two.

Ironically, it was a job that in many ways transformed me and which even today, fifteen years later, still influences me. I remember thumbing through the jobs section in the newspaper (remember those?). The sad part was that I was not really qualified for much. However, I did stumble across a listing for a mountain biking and hiking guide at a local resort. That sounded fun and appealing! I sent in my resume.

My "interview" entailed tagging along on a two-hour hike with other guides. Afterwards we put the packs away and got out a number of mountain bikes for a tour. For two hours I tagged along and had a great time. Those are my kind of interviews.

When the ride was over, I was offered the job. It was a spectacular five-year run.

I was fortunate in many ways. I was able to provide for my family while I planted a church, secured amazing and affordable health insurance, and learned so many lessons along the way. On top of that, the kinds of daily interactions that I had with other guides as well as guests transformed me. After hiking and mountain biking with celebrities, high-level CEOs, and the one-percenters, I learned quickly that I can talk with anyone and everyone.

These are the kinds of life lessons that can't be learned in school or through classroom training, regardless of how extensive and intensive it is. For me, it was the first time that I began thinking about the topics addressed in this book. How could we best prepare church planters for missionary service in a way that not only imparts the essential skills needed for planting, but also the foundational skills for doing something that could bring value to the community that we're planting in? In other words, how do we train church planters to be social entrepreneurs?

Infusing Social Entrepreneurship Into Church Planting

Social entrepreneurship is a hot topic right now. Countless books, blogs, and articles detail the concept and its meteoric rise. So what is the fuss? Why is it important for church planting? Ruth Shapiro notes, "The term *social entrepreneur* was originally coined by Bill Drayton of Ashoka in the early 1980s to refer to someone with the passions and focus of an entrepreneur who tackles a social challenge."[1] TOMS founder Blake Mycoskie expands on this in his book *Start Something That Matters*:

> There is something different in the air these days: I feel it when I talk to business leaders, give speeches at high school and college campuses, and engage in conversation with fellow patrons at coffee shops. People are hungry for success-- that's nothing new. What's changed is the definition of that success. Increasingly, the quest is not the same as the quest for status and money. The definition has broadened to include contributing something to the world and living and working on one's own terms.[2]

Not only can we train and equip church planters, but we can also give them the tools, exposure, and knowledge to start businesses *that matter* in their communities. We do recognize that there really is a very similar, almost identical, ethos between church planters and entrepreneurs. Nate Morsches picks up on this in his article "Why Church Planters and Entrepreneurs Are So Similar":

> In the church, we don't want to admit that Church Planters and Entrepreneurs are

---

[1] Shapiro, *The Real Problem Solvers*, 3.
[2] Mycoskie, *Start Something That Matters*, 18-19.

similar. We have this stigma that says that if it's business-like, then it's automatically unspiritual or un-church-like. It's simply not true. Obviously, they have major differences, too––one expands the tool God is using to bless the nations, spread the gospel, and show his manifold wisdom, and the other expands a business for making money. [...] An entrepreneur and a church planter require the same talents and gifts from God. There is so much they have in common when it comes to the work itself.[3]

The pertinent question then is this: how do we train church planters to not only be entrepreneurs, but social entrepreneurs?

No one expects seminaries to give you *actual* practical skills and tools to earn a living and provide for your family. But what if *while* in seminary, there were options to take parallel tracks? Meaning, what if while you were working on your MDiv, you also had to choose a track such as launching a marketing company, roasting coffee, establishing a mountain-biking trail alliance, starting an urban gardening co-op, creating a riparian habitat restoration advocacy group, or launching a non-profit focusing on economic development? Niche and nuanced? You bet. The point? To give church planting

---

[3] Morsches, "Why Church Planters and Entrepreneurs Are So Similar," para. 1-3.

missionaries tools and skills to assist them in the church planting process.

I know this isn't for everyone, but I also know that for *most* church planters, this would be invaluable. You see, for every church planter moving to your city with $250,000 to $850,000 in the bank or pledged, there are ten church planters moving with a dream, a passion, and a calling—and *no* money. What if these church-planting "99 percenters" came with skills, tools, and a know-how to not only sustain themselves long-term, but also to create missionary pathways to connect with and love the communities they're moving to? I know, it sounds crazy. It's almost so far-fetched that it's biblical.

What's missing in our church planting training? *Practical skills and tools.* That *while* we train planters in disciple-making and creating new churches from scratch, we also give them the essential skills and tools needed to carry them long-term.

That then creates a whole new world of possibilities for church planting. It also can and will free up church planters to consider less desirable and down-trodden communities. One of the unspoken conversations church planters have with themselves, but are too afraid to say out loud or with others, comes down to the geographic and socio-economic considerations for planting. Most planters steer away from economically declining communities and instead opt for growing, livable, and middle-class (and higher) communities to plant in. When the rationale behind funding for planting says that your new church should sustain your salary after three to five years, then why would any planter plant in an economically depressed community? You may *never* plant a church that could pay your salary— nor should that be your motive.

I know these are the thoughts we're too afraid to share with others. But we *all* have them.

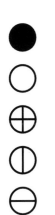

10

WHO ARE YOU?

+++++++++++++++

The chapter speaks to a subject that I think about continuously and have written about in snippets over the last number of years. A few pages here, a few pages there, an occasional chapter, and so on, as I wrestle with it in my own life. Writing helps me process my own internal dialogue. I write to think.

My missionary calling came before my formal education or training. All I knew was that when God rescued and redeemed me, out of gratitude and worship I needed to in turn relinquish my life to him in service. As time went on and educational and occupational opportunities came my way, that early sense of calling became the filter through which most (if not all) of my major life decisions have passed.

Vocation vs. Occupation

I have read a lot and have refined my language over time in addressing this topic. Early on I learned to differentiate between *vocation* and *occupation*. According to Dictionary.com, "vocation" can be defined as "a divine call to God's service or to the Christian life."[1] This applies to *all* Christians. In contrast, occupation is "a

---

[1] Dictionary.com, LLC, "Vocation."

person's usual or principal work or business, especially as a means of earning a living."[2] This is how I distinguish between the two, so that at least in own mind, they are complementary and concise.

My vocation, what God has called me to do, is missions, ministry, service. That has not changed, nor will it ever change. I have thrown my whole life into this deep sense of calling. It has shaped and defined who I am and what I do. However, what *has* changed and is fluid is my occupation, how I "earn a living." That has been in flux since coming to faith in Christ. When I was in college and studying, training, and being equipped for a life of vocational ministry, I had *a lot* of jobs—working in the college kitchen, landscaping, sales clerk at a bookstore, etc. My occupation was a moving target, but my vocation never changed.

Not every Christian will be called to live out their vocation in full-time "Christian ministry." For most, it is about living out this universal vocation in whatever occupation for which they are best wired, gifted, and suited. We're all called to give our lives to Christ in full-time service, but that doesn't necessarily have to mean choosing a faith-based job or career. There is a myriad of ways that Christians can serve their Lord, and none is better or superior.

---

[2] Dictionary.com, LLC, "Occupation."

After college, I entered full-time work in a local church as a youth pastor. Did my vocation change? No, not a bit. But my occupation did. It was neither better nor worse than when I was laying fifty-pound blocks or building retaining walls. How I earned my money was the only thing that changed. As a landscaper, I would share the gospel willingly with anyone who would listen. As a clerk in a bookstore, I would spend my breaks sharing Jesus. I was as riveted to my calling in those jobs as I was as a youth pastor.

This does not mean that we don't learn over time to navigate life and position ourselves to more fully and effectively live out our calling. But in my mind, there was no difference between being paid to be a church planter and being paid to be a mountain-biking guide. No matter what the job, I was living out my vocation. On the trail I would share the gospel when opportunity arose, and at times I would be a listening ear to stories of pain, disappointment, addiction, and brokenness. I would pray with these people. Later that same day, I'd be in a coffee shop prepping for a sermon or working on small-group materials. Both occupations were subordinate to my vocation.

We may not like to admit it, but this conversation is highly nuanced and cultural. For example, it is assumed that pastors in white churches in the US are full-time. Conversely, most of the black or Hispanic churches that I know of have pastors who work full-time outside the church to earn a living. For many minority pastors, their vocation is to lead local churches which may or may not be able to pay them. But even though their occupation might be outside their church, that does not diminish their vocation.

I am incredibly privileged to be in a position where from time to time my vocation and my occupation have merged into one "job" (although that is not the case right now, as I'll explain later). I understand that on some level, that is the result of the larger cultural narrative of *white privilege*. However, for most of my adult life, my vocation never really provided as much financially as my growing family needed, which is why I have also needed to work in various jobs on the side, as well as launch a couple of business ventures.

I wonder how or even if Father Kino ever thought or talked about such things. Obviously, his time, context, and circumstances differed greatly from today. The throne of Spain paid for his missionary endeavors and he was paired up with the Spanish military. Everywhere Kino traveled, he was flanked by military personnel. Not quite the same experience that our church planters have today. But church planters today don't worry about warring Apaches raiding villages or intertribal conflict as he did.

When People Don't Understand You

This all ties in to how we view our ministry roles on this continent versus overseas. For many the difference is enormous. This is even evident in raising missionary support. Since I've worked for missions organizations and attempted to raise funds to engage in missionary work throughout North America, I have come alongside a number of others seeking to do the same. Unfortunately, for many who are transitioning back to the US or Canada after having spent an extended time overseas as missionaries, the storyline is all too familiar.

While these people were serving sacrificially overseas, they received ample support. However, once the Lord led them back to North America to engage in missions here, they saw a significant drop in support. It seems that even those large "sending" churches didn't understand the need for "missions" in North America. Thus, support for these returning missionaries dwindled. Some have had to leave their ministries altogether in search of the income they needed to support their families.

The dichotomy is clear: missions is work that's carried out *somewhere else* and therefore worthy of being supported, whereas ministry that's carried out *here* somehow does not need to be supported. This to some degree complicates what we mean by calling, vocation, and occupation when geography and international borders are factored in. It also elevates the need for us to think more deeply about how we view ourselves: Are we religious professionals or are we missionaries? Or are they one and the same?

Who Are You?

How do you see yourself? Unfortunately, if you self-identify as a missionary, that can elicit puzzled looks when you also say that you live in Boise, Omaha, Kansas City, or Miami. For us, it was a challenge when fundraising to explain that we are indeed raising missionary support, but that we're not leaving Portland. Many prospective donors assume that self-identifying as a missionary and raising support means that our destination is somewhere beyond the borders of our country.

But don't we need more missionaries here? Don't we need people who live, think, and act like missionaries here more than we need more "religious professionals?" As we've seen, context dictates that we immediately begin to shift our thinking in a missions direction. The beauty is that once we begin thinking this way—when we begin to see ourselves as missionaries rather than as pastors and church workers—the door for creativity and innovation begins to open. Make sense?

As I mentioned earlier, my current occupation is multi-faceted. I have the privilege of working part-time for and with The Table Network. I also run and operate my own coffee-roasting company, as well as teach at several universities. I'm not a full-time professor, but my workload certainly is.

One of the classes I teach is called "Spirituality, Character, and Service." Interestingly my students this semester are a cohort of business majors. Their program deals with finances, business practices, human resources, and the like. And then they're thrust into my class, which really goes to the heart of calling and vocation.

This course is a gut-check because from the beginning, the question I ask is, "Who are *you*?" One of the books we're reading together is *Let Your Life Speak* by Parker Palmer. He asks the kinds of questions that make you squirm, but his own vulnerability gives you permission to simply lay all of your cards on the table.

Parker contends that this sense of vocation is really about understanding who we are and what we're drawn to. Like many, he asserts that vocation is not simply for "religious workers." We all have a vocation. As I shared earlier, I believe that our first and primary vocation is to follow Christ and to live for him and his purposes. I also believe that he has uniquely wired, gifted, and called us for a "secondary" purpose:

> Vocation does not come from willfulness. It comes from listening. Vocation does not mean a goal that I pursue. It means a calling that I hear. Before I can tell my life what I want to do with it, I must listen to my life telling me who I am. I must listen for truths and values at the heart of my own identity, not

the standards by which I *must* live––but the standards by which I cannot help but live if I am living my own life.[3]

Later in the book, Palmer writes about wearing other people's masks when it comes to vocation. What did God create us for? As we live for him, *how* do we do that in a career that is not only God-honoring, but also gives life to our souls? I'm not a great leader and therefore I found pastoral ministry soul-sucking. However, I love planning, strategizing, and creating, which means the most satisfying ministry roles I've been in were when I could do those things. For me, starting a publishing company and then a coffee company were all about creating.

Parker says vocation "at its deepest level is, 'This is something I can't not do, for reasons I'm unable to explain to anyone else and don't fully understand myself but that are nonetheless compelling.'"[4] You see, vocation (to borrow his use of the word) is like birds migrating from Canada to Central America and then back again depending on the season. We don't know why or how they know to do this, but they do. There's something hard-wired within them that draws them south for the winter and north for the summer.

For inexplicable reasons, we simply gravitate towards some things and away from most others.

---

[3] Palmer, *Let Your Life Speak*, 4-5.
[4] Ibid., 25.

I love learning, reading, writing, and teaching. It is no wonder I love academia. It has an intrinsic pull. The same goes with creating, new ventures, and the like, which fits perfectly in the realm of church planting. What energizes me is creating strategies and mobilizing planters for places that are off the beaten path. I want to see churches planted across the hinterlands, the places *most* church planters shy away from. That comes from my love for obscurity and anonymity and is why I follow small-college football. I'd rather go to a football game to see Western New Mexico University in Silver City, New Mexico, than watch the Oregon Ducks or the USC Trojans.

Too often we're pressured to live out what others believe is our true calling. Maybe our parents urged us to go to law school, become a doctor, take over the family firm, pursue a career as a high school teacher, or be a senior pastor. But who are you *really*? What gives your soul life and nourishment? The foundational premise is that above all, you need to be honest with yourself. Stop living other people's lives and start living the unique life for which God created you.

> What a long time it can take to become the person one has always been! How often in the process we mask ourselves in faces that are not our own, how much dissolving and shaking of ego we must endure before we discover our deep identity—the true self within every human

being that is the seed of authentic vocation.[5]

For too long, I've worn other people's masks. Now I know who I am. Now I know what I love doing. Now more than ever I am free to simply be me, to live the life for which God has wired me and gifted me. How about you?

This is the epicenter of church planting and social entrepreneurship. The authentic "you" is a gift to the community you're seeking to love for the sake of the gospel.

---

[5] Ibid., 9.

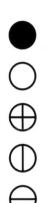

11

PULLING THE PIECES TOGETHER

++++++++++++++

I find it interesting that although most of my formal education has revolved around pastoral ministries, church planting, and the like, I've ended up teaching a lot about economics. As I began to transition away from "occupational ministry" and while I was working on a PhD in urban studies, I sat through several classes on economics. Some focused on the current landscape and others examined the history of capitalism. I couldn't help but translate everything I learned back to the world of church planting and missions. That's when it all began to click.

This past week, I had one of my classes ("Bicycles, Equity, and Race: Urban Mobility in Portland") do a bike count along North Williams Avenue. We stopped first at Legacy Emanuel Hospital to visit the exhibit detailing the history of the local neighborhood. Not only did students learn about the history of Albina as a stand-alone town that Portland eventually swallowed up, but also the plight of the African American community. In particular, the students learned about what transpired following the Vanport flood in 1948 which displaced thousands of blacks, the hundreds of homes that were demolished under the banner of "urban renewal," and the ongoing gentrification that has forever reshaped the neighborhood.

I had the students walk in teams from the hospital up the parallel streets of North Williams and Vancouver as they counted pedestrians and cyclists, noted their ethnicity, helmet usage, gender, and so on. I also had them check out a few stores along the corridor to find out who they're targeting in terms of their customer base, and more. They charted everything in writing and turned their papers in to me. Yesterday we debriefed what we saw and experienced.

While we could easily explain what we saw— newer bike lanes, lots of people on bikes, scores of pedestrians, explosive mixed-use development growth, and the like—the tricky part was answering the "why" question. You see, whereas this part of Portland had been home to our African American community, walking it today reveals a different present reality. Almost everyone we saw was white. We read the displays at the exhibit in the hospital, learned about the changes in the neighborhood, and saw those first-hand, but the bigger question is: Why?

This is where economics comes in.

While there were many factors affecting neighborhood succession, including redlining, discrimination, and so on, one of the most significant changes had to do with economics. I bring this up, because the undercurrents that have reshaped American inner cities and our suburbs all come back to this economic shift. *And* that in turn dovetails into this notion of social entrepreneurship as related to church planting.

It is precisely this economic climate which creates the conditions for talking about this topic. Again, on many levels this is nothing new. Start-ups have been around since the first businesses came into existence. In fact, they're nearly as old as human history, in particular urban history.

What is different, though, is the unique nature of our current economy. There has been a confluence of advancements in technology with a shift to a post-industrial or post-manufacturing economy. While this book does not allow us the space to get into all the details, there are a few cursory outcomes worth mentioning.

Economics 101

A comparative analysis between a Fordist (i.e., manufacturing or industrial) versus a Post-Fordist economy reveals that the differences are more profound than simply how goods are produced and the resulting impact on our GDP. While we are certainly a "post-everything" economy, that certainly does not mean we don't produce manufactured or industrial goods at all. Automation as well as the ability to produce cheaper goods internationally simply means that we no longer rely on it to drive our economy. It is here that the creative or knowledge-based economy fills the gap. This is also why we've shifted from former industrial powerhouses like

Cleveland and Detroit to new economic powerhouses such as the Bay Area.

The current economic climate allows for much greater autonomy, flexibility, and the integration of work, living, and socializing places. It's not about punching the time clock at the start and end of an eight- or ten-hour shift. Instead, with the aid of technology, both work and *where* we work are flexible. These are prime conditions for the church planting social entrepreneur to step onto the stage. Rather than segmenting "church life" from "work life," there's now the freedom and the opportunity more than ever before to combine the two somewhat seamlessly. Not only that, but the conventional means by which church planters and missionaries fundraise appears to be going through another shift.

Common Good Businesses

Recently, I took that same class to a new non-profit bike and coffee shop. It focuses on training and employing homeless teens. They're taught how to be a barista or bike mechanic, paired up with a mentor, and then the shop hires them as paid interns. One long-term goal is to give them the skills and tools to make a career in these industries.

Towards the end our time at Braking Cycles, the director mentioned something that stuck out. She also works for an organization that helps transitional youth. For nearly thirty years, it has been fundraising and applying for grants through various foundations. What makes this new shop unique is that its goal is to become sustainable and turn a profit.

That is a decisive shift—moving away from dependency on outside organizations and donors to self-sufficiency by providing a public service such as quality coffee and bike repair. My immediate response was, "That's it! That's precisely what this book is about!" That hour-long meeting captured the essence of this book: combining social entrepreneurship with ministry.

That's not to say that grants and donors are not important. Often they can help jumpstart something. But what we need to think about is long-term sustainability. In every community where we're planting churches, what if we also launched businesses that (a) provided for our families, (b) created natural inroads into the community, and (c) blessed our communities? That "blessing" could be in the form of services provided, products created, and/or new jobs incubated. In this scenario, everyone wins, the church planter *and* the community, regardless of whether it's in the city or a small town.

While the business climate is constantly in flux, we are still in the throes of the postindustrial economy. I tell my students repeatedly that they will earn their livelihood post-graduation by using their mind and creativity rather than by some form of physical labor. While we're now several decades deep into this transition, we continue to see how this unfolds especially in light of changing technologies.

I know that many of us are proud of the mantra "shop local." In the beginning we all seemed to love Amazon.com, but now more and more people are becoming disillusioned as this giant corporation gobbles up others. But as a Prime member, how can you beat free two-day shipping and prices that are better than almost anything you can find locally? I may enjoy shopping local when it is convenient, but most days it is simply *more* convenient to buy online. Guilty as charged.

However, more than that, it is also a reflection of what is changing in culture and business, and why. For the purposes of this conversation, it also means that because of the growth of social media and technology, the semi-entrepreneurial person can take a crack at launching a new business, carve out an identity and a following, and actually make it work! I'm not simply talking about Silicon Valley start-ups, but regular people like you and me.

As I shared before, I've ventured into starting two businesses. And because both required growing an online footprint through social media and online sales, I am constantly learning about this online world and the implications for starting businesses. In terms of this book, the most important implication for church planters is that because we live in this postindustrial economy, aided by these technological advances, even those in rural America can start a business and distribute their products globally. They can even *compete* globally.

More Unwritten Rules of Church Planting

Since I'm more drawn to the creative side than the business side, I'm conscious of my own limitations as a businessman. But the fact remains that more than ever before, it is possible to combine church planting with launching businesses, and to do both well. When I receive pushback from this idea of combining church planting and start-ups, it is usually from those within an attractional church-planting framework. They say it takes so much time, energy, and money to pull off a weekly worship gathering that the church planter can't afford to also start a business. My response is usually along the lines of, "Is that what we'd do overseas?"

Meaning that we have, as I've shared before, invented different rules for those we deem church planters (here) and those we label missionaries (there). That's why I advocate that, on the contrary, we need to think and act like missionaries *here*. What is normative for *there* needs to be normative for *here*. When we begin abandoning the labels and the "unwritten rules of church planting," we will no longer be slaves to "how church planting *should* be done."

Recently I was on a phone call with a church planter who had just relocated to a small mining town in Arizona. Three months into his move, he was frustrated and even a little disillusioned. He was beginning to question his calling as he ran into one closed door after another. He tried to secure volunteer as well as paid positions involving addiction recovery in the local prison, and teaching about sexual-assault awareness in the schools. In a moment of desperation, he instead launched his own non-profit so he could do what he felt called and compelled to do, as well as give himself a platform and a legal covering.

He told me he was feeling somewhat guilty about having done this because it wasn't within the "normal" activities of a church planter. I told him these were *precisely* the kind of activities he needed to be involved in. I cast the vision for planting under this "Intrepid" motif and explained how this freed him up to love, serve, and meet the needs in his community. During the course of our conversation he began crying as I tried to affirm him. He was on the right track!

How many other church planters are *out there* feeling encumbered by all these written and unwritten rules of church planting? You see needs everywhere in your community that starting a worship gathering will simply not meet. It's not that people don't need Jesus. They *do*. The community needs to see the gospel lived out and presented in a compelling way; but it also needs to see a turnaround in the local economy. The best news from our perspective is that we don't have to do one or the other. We can do *both*.

This past weekend, we headed to the Oregon coast for the day. As spectacular and breathtaking as it is, I've become a bit bored by it. I think part of my boredom is that we repeatedly end up hitting the same well-trafficked places. When relatives visit us from out of state, we always make a trip to the coast and visit the same beaches, seemingly along with half of Portland. As a result, whenever we speak of going to the coast, I squirm.

But this time was different. I decided we needed to explore more of the coast and small towns that we hadn't visited yet. Which we did.

It rained the entire trip. Record-breaking rainfall. The wind blew like a tempest. The waves crashed violently along the craggy coastline. The fog along the coast made the dense forest even more brooding. Every time we got out of the car, we were soon drenched, even in rain gear.

But it was the best trip I have ever had to the coast.

We explored small town after small town, visiting local thrift stores, coffee shops, candy stores, and more. Some towns were much more impacted by tourism than others. Some had hot real estate markets while others were struggling. All throughout the day, I couldn't help but see everything through this "Intrepid" filter. It was exhilarating. Oftentimes we see "depressed" communities that leave us depressed. We think to ourselves, "This place is gross! Who'd want to live there?" But it doesn't have to be that way.

We know that Jesus is the Messiah, which frees us up from any messianic complexes. We're not here to save any community. Instead we see hope. Potential. That does not diminish the need for hard work and a long-term perspective, but with how things are changing, economically downtrodden communities are not being left for dead. All is not hopeless for these communities in the hinterlands.

One of the big undercurrents in all of this revolves around the seismic economic shifts and the implications of geography. With coastal cities and states capturing mobile capital and talent, the heartland is becoming a wasteland of sorts. However, even on the periphery of the more successful regions of the US, this boom and growing wealth is not being distributed equally, as my recent trip to the Oregon coast revealed. Growing cities are the winners, leaving in their wake depressed communities. And that includes both rural towns as well as neighborhoods within cities that are on a downward spiral.

I started this book off with Father Kino for a reason. To me, he becomes almost the patron saint of *Intrepid* and struggling communities everywhere, whether urban or rural. What if he thought like church planters do today? He would've seen the half-naked Pimas, the inhospitable and foreboding desert, and headed back to the comforts of European cities. Instead he rolled up his sleeves, girded his robe, and dove in for the long term.

The thing about obscurity is that it is, well, obscure. While we had heard of Kino, it wasn't until his autobiography was rediscovered in a dusty library archive in Mexico that we uncovered the truth about this padre on horseback. Until then, much of his work and life had been a mystery. He could have used his education, his gifts, and his drive to succeed at anything in life, but instead he used them for the betterment of a previously unknown Native American tribe in the far reaches of the Sonoran Desert.

We love and follow a Savior who left behind unimaginable joy and power and majesty so that he could live and walk among us. To grow up in the home of a tradesman in a small, nondescript town, to suffer with us, and to die on the cross for the betterment of all humanity to the glory of the Father.

Kino followed in the footsteps of Jesus. He left everything to travel across an ocean, endure a bone-bleaching desert, and suffer with and for the Pimas. He would ultimately die in this foreign land that he grew to call home. May we too give ourselves fully to our neighborhoods, towns, and cities.

Connecting with Intrepid

The mission of Intrepid is to partner with and mobilize local churches to plant new churches across North America in under-reached and off-the-beaten-path communities, particularly communities that have been in economic decline and are transitioning to revitalize their local economy. To see churches planted where people come to Christ and the community is lifted through new businesses, non-profits, job creation, and more.

Intrepid + The Table Network

To connect with us you can join one of our cohorts where we collectively study and work through such topics as community and economic development, church planting, business as mission, social entrepreneurship, justice and disciple-making. Go to www.intrepidmissions.com or www.thetablenetwork.com.

Bibliography

Barrier, Roger. *Listening to the Voice of God*.
Minneapolis: Bethany House, 1998.

Briggs, Alan. *Staying is the New Going: Choosing
to Love Where God Places You*. Colorado
Springs: NavPress, 2015.

Bolton, Herbert. *The Padre on Horseback: A
Sketch of Eusebio Francisco Kino, S.J. Apostle
to the Pimas*. Chicago: Loyola University Press,
1982.

Cole, Matt "One Hell of a Party: Northern British
Columbia's Bike-Powered Renaissance."
Freehub Magazine 6.4 (2015) 63-76.

Dictionary.com, LLC. "Occupation."
Dictionary.com. Online:
Dictionary.com/browse/occupation.

_____. "Vocation." *Dictionary.com*. Online:
Dictionary.com/browse/vocation.

Fogelson, Robert M. *Downtown: Its Rise and Fall,
1880-1950*. New Haven: Yale University Press,
2001.

Investopia, LLC. "Social Entrepreneur." *Investopia*.
Online:
http://www.investopedia.com/terms/s/social-
entrepreneur.asp.

Lamberton, Ken. *Dry River: Stories of Life, Death,
and Redemption on the Santa Cruz*. Tucson:
The University of Arizona Press, 2011.

Morsches, Nate. "The Apostle Paul Was Not a Pastor, and You Might Not Really Be One Either." *The Borough* (February 4, 2016). Online: https://www.theboroughonline.com/the-apostle-paul-was-not-a-pastor-and-you-might-not-really-be-one-either.

———. "Why Church Planters and Entrepreneurs Are So Similar." *The Borough* (February 29, 2016). Online: https://www.theboroughonline.com/why-church+planters-and-entrepreneurs-are-so-similar.

Mycoskie, Blake. *Start Something That Matters.* New York: Spiegel & Grau, 2012.

Palmer, Parker J. *Let Your Life Speak: Listening for the Voice of Vocation.* San Francisco: Jossey-Bass, 2000.

Reséndez, Andrés. *A Land So Strange: The Epic Journey of Cabeza de Vaca.* New York: Basic Books, 2007.

Semuels, Alana. "The Graying of Rural America." *The Atlantic* (June 2, 2016). Online: https://www.theatlantic.com/business/archive/2016/06/the-graying-of-rural-america/485159/.

Shapiro, Ruth A. *The Real Problem Solvers: Social Entrepreneurs in America.* Stanford: Stanford Business Books, 2013.

Siegler, Kirk. "Doctor Shortage In Rural Arizona Sparks Another Crisis in 'Forgotten America.'" *NPR* (July 14, 2017. Online:

https://www.npr.org/sections/health-shots/2017/07/14/535792864/doctor-shortage-in-rural-arizona-sparks-another-crisis-in-forgotten-america.

Sigler, Thomas. "Is There Such Thing as 'Rural' Gentrification?" *Planetizen* (February 21, 2012). Online: https://www.planetizen.com/node/54684.

Wikimedia Foundation, Inc. "Eusebio Kino." *Wikipedia*. Online: https://en.wikipedia.org/wiki/Eusebio_Kino.

_____. "Social Entrepreneurship." *Wikipedia*. Online: https://en.wikipedia.org/wiki/Social_entrepreneurship.

Wright, Christopher J.H. *The Mission of God's People: A Biblical Theology of the Church's Mission*. Grand Rapids: Zondervan, 2010.

Woodard, Colin. *American Nations: A History of the Eleven Rival Regional Cultures of North America*. New York: Penguin, 2011.

About the Author

Sean Benesh lives in the Pacific Northwest and is a professor, author, coffee roaster, and leads an initiative called Intrepid for The Table Network.

With a post-Christian society looming over the Western horizon, many church leaders and members race for the magic bullet. Ironically, it's the freedom from this race, made available to us through the gospel, that invites us to embrace an ancient, minimalist approach resonating amongst those who are uninterested in the church. Slow Down is a tangible look at this ancient way for our present time.

AVAILABLE NOW ON AMAZON

For more info visit us at thetablenetwork.com

INTREPID COHORTS

COMMUNITY DEVELOPMENT
+ CHURCH PLANTING

In the world of ministry and church planting, under-reached and off-the-beaten-path communities (both urban and rural) are often overlooked due to popular financial support structures. But what if you could start a sustainable business that contributes to the development of your community and brings support to your family all while extending the freedom and family of Jesus to those you meet?

Knowing the easy disconnect between information and transformation, we've embraced the Hebraic learning approach we see in Jesus. Rather than help people think their way into a new way of acting (the Hellenistic approach), He invited the disciples to come act their way into a new way of thinking. To that end, we designed a 12 month journey to help you develop the foundation and framework you need to combine community development with Good News.

For more info: thetablenetwork.com/social-entrepreneur-cohort

THE SLOW DOWN is a podcast hosted by everyday people who are navigating life and discipleship by the seat of their pants and the grace of God. We take an unfiltered look at how the finished work of Jesus has set us free from the exhausting madness of trying to fix our lives and the lives of others. Listen in on our ongoing dialogue concerning the simple, but rather hard realities that accompany the practice of extending the freedom and family of Jesus to those we encounter.

AVAILABLE NOW ON iTUNES, GOOGLE MUSIC, STITCHER, PODBEAN, AND MORE.

For more info visit us at thetablenetwork.com

START TELLING A DIFFERENT STORY

The Slow Down Workshop takes a serious look at the
current spiritual climate in the West while taking a deep
dive into the scriptures to examine what the early
disciples were saying and doing while the world was
being turned upside down. Over the course of a handful
of hours you'll hear teaching, participate in discussion,
and have time to reflect on your own life and context
regarding the spread of the Message, Medium, and
Mission of Jesus to those uninterested in the church.
Our hope is that this workshop experience will help you
to find rest, slow down, and begin inviting others into
the freedom and family of Jesus.

We can help you host a workshop at your house, in your
neighborhood or for your church.

For more info visit us at thetablenetwork.com

Made in the USA
Columbia, SC
09 July 2020

13519380R00104